Aloha To Mark & Angelia
& Buona Cucina
Casa Castagnola
Honolulu, 1995

COOKING ITALIAN IN HAWAII

George Sabato
"Cass"
Castagnola

To my wife,
Ruth,
who made
this book
possible,
and to the
people of
Hawaii,
who
proved the
experts wrong

COOKING ITALIAN IN HAWAII

George Sabato "Cass" Castagnola

EDITOR
George Engebretson

DESIGNER
Elsa Carl

FOOD PHOTOGRAPHER
Rae J. Huo

WATERMARK
PUBLISHING

© 1991
All rights reserved.

No part of this book may be
reproduced in any form
or by any electronic or
mechanical means, including
information storage and retrieval
systems, without permission
in writing from the publisher,
except for brief passages
quoted in reviews.

Library of Congress Catalog Number:
91-066826

ISBN 0-9631154-0-5

Printed in Singapore

Watermark Publishing
1311 Kalakaua Avenue
Suite A
Honolulu, Hawaii
96826

CONTENTS

- 6   Foreword
- 7   Introduction
- 9   The Basics
- 21   Appetizers
- 31   Pizza
- 41   Pasta
- 55   Poultry
- 63   Seafood
- 77   Meats
- 97   Vegetables
- 103   Salads
- 109   Soups
- 117   Desserts
- 126   Index
- 128   Credits

FOREWORD

When is a drive to Manoa Valley like a trip to Italy? When you're dining at Castagnola's, a one-of-a-kind restaurant in suburban Honolulu. Although those two places are literally a world apart, "Cass" Castagnola's restaurant never fails to serve truly authentic Italian fare.

But just as important is the aloha Cass has for Hawaii and his enthusiasm for contributing to our island community. At Castagnola's, he makes everyone feel like *ohana*, or family — providing an atmosphere that guests enjoy right along with the cuisine.

That same feeling is captured in *Cooking Italian in Hawaii*. If you're seeking delightful Italian dining, Castagnola's is the place. If you're looking to take that experience into your own kitchen, this is the cookbook.

Hawaii's food, like its people, is a mix of many different cultures. And thanks to Cass, that mix now includes world-class Italian cuisine.

Komo mai e 'ai Italiano! Come and eat Italian!

Danny Kaleikini
Hawaii's Ambassador of Aloha

INTRODUCTION

It's a long way from Hawaii to the streets of Naples or the fields of San Marzano. In fact, it's a long way from Hawaii to just about anywhere. These beautiful islands are the most remote landfall in the world.

When we opened Castagnola's, our restaurant in suburban Honolulu, this location in the middle of the Pacific Ocean was our biggest challenge. Years of experience had taught me and my wife, Ruth, that the key to successful *cucina* is using the freshest, top-quality ingredients — no matter how far you have to go to find them.

But back in 1984, we found skeptics more plentiful than pinto beans in Pasta Fagiole. Bringing in fresh ingredients from halfway around the world, they said, would never pay off. "Don't waste your money!" the experts told us. "Honolulu's lunch and dinner crowd won't appreciate the difference anyway."

Together with the people of Hawaii, we've proved the experts wrong. Today, Castagnola's receives excellent reviews from food writers from all over the world. Even more important, our restaurant has been voted one of Hawaii's top ten restaurants the past four years in a row — by the people themselves.

Why? Because people know quality when they taste it. Because people can tell when you don't cut corners. Because in a world of preservatives and color enhancers and pre-cooked meals, people are hungry for fresh, wholesome, natural foods.

The fact is, you can cook Italian the way it was meant to be cooked, even if you're doing it halfway around the world from the piggeries of Parma or the pasta factories of Abruzzi. And if we can do it right here in Hawaii, then so can you, whether you hang your apron in Hilo or Pocatello.

The purpose of this book is to share some of the secrets of traditional Italian cooking — using the freshest, top-quality ingredients, the right tools and some of our most popular recipes. In these pages, we'll translate what we do at Castagnola's into great results right in your own kitchen.

One way or another, I've been in the kitchen just about all my life.

It's also a long way from Hawaii to New Jersey, but that's where I started my love affair with good cooking — learning culinary secrets from my Neapolitan father and my French mother.

Before moving to Hawaii, I owned a restaurant in Wallington, New Jersey, near Giants Stadium, where we served everything from "killer" chili to shrimp cooked in ale to sauteed carduni — and all to a truly diverse clientele. That first Castagnola's taught us a lot about different individual tastes. Everything was fresh, we made our own bread, sauces and condiments, our hamburger was ground at the restaurant daily, and we'd slice your steak from the sirloin right at your table.

Today's Castagnola's is a very different kind of cafe. Located in the beautiful Honolulu neighborhood of Manoa Valley, it's an intimate, traditional Italian restaurant, where the personal touch is alive and well. One important feature at Castagnola's is our deli, with fine products from imported extra virgin olive oil to fresh-made sausage available over the counter. If you have difficulty locating any of the ingredients called for in this book, chances are we carry them in our own deli. One other tip: our phone lines at Castagnola's are always open to field questions about recipes or ingredients.

And now, Castagnola's has company. In the same spirit of the neighborhood bistro, we've opened a second Honolulu restaurant — Castagnola's Italian Lanai — on the edge of Waikiki. The Lanai lets us bring real Italian cooking closer to Waikiki's many residents, as well as to the resort area's millions of annual visitors.

But whether in Manoa or Waikiki, the Castagnola's philosophy remains the same: to serve the finest possible product to a clientele that appreciates the difference. In a way, good cooking is like any other quality product; you have to use the best raw materials to get the best results. To make a handsome dining room table, you use the best hardwood you can find — not plywood. To make a designer evening gown, you use silk — not polyester.

And to create a truly memorable Italian dinner, you use the right ingredients. Pasta made with artesian mineral water from the Abruzzi region. Plum tomatoes from the vineyards of San Marzano. Extra virgin olive oil from the orchards of Tuscany. Parmesan cheese and prosciutto from Parma. Buffalo mozzarella from Naples. Vegetables, herbs and spices from natural gardens. Locally grown chicken and fresh fish pulled from the bountiful fishing grounds we have right here in Hawaii. The list goes on and on.

Home cooking, of course, has limitations. A volume restaurant operation enjoys certain advantages which just aren't available to the individual shopper. At Castagnola's, for instance, we import our plum tomatoes from San Marzano by the containerload — more than 900 cases a year — and alternate those shipments with huge lots of extra virgin olive oil. And we bring in weekly shipments of chilled meats, carefully inspecting each side of beef before accepting it to become Veal Sorrentino or Beef Braciole.

But there are also many things you can do to ensure the freshest possible ingredients. In the pages ahead, you'll find plenty of new cooking ideas, suggested ingredients substitutions and — most important of all — shopping hints. Successful cuisine, after all, begins not in the kitchen but at the market.

To do it right, cooking Italian in Hawaii — or anywhere — means going that extra mile. It means finding the best ingredients and using the best tools — for freshness, for nutrition, and for just plain good eating.

Aloha and mahalo,

George Cass Castagnola

George Sabato "Cass" Castagnola

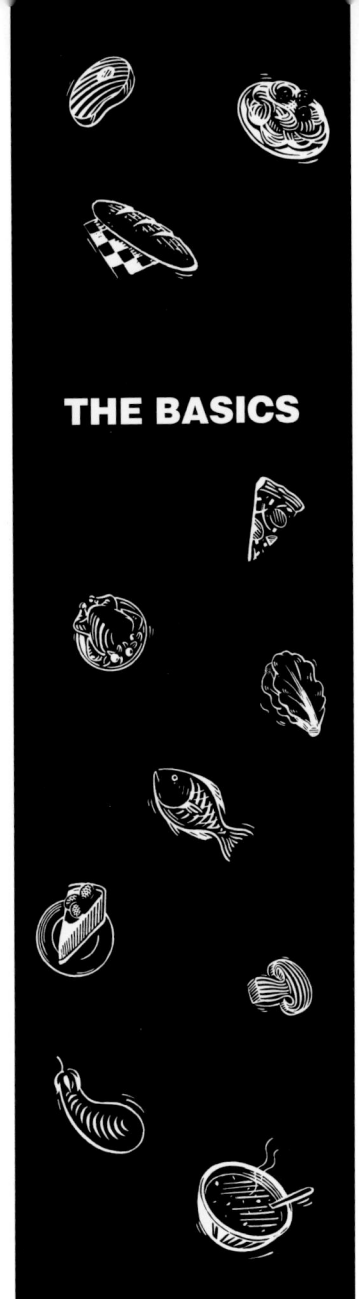

THE BASICS

On a winding mountain road in Fara San Martino, Italy, big trucks careen through the curves, loaded with flour going uphill and carrying pasta on the way back down. Up on the mountain's slope are the manufacturers of the world's best pasta — great big beautiful plants far from any large city or industrial center.

Why go to such great lengths to build and service such remote plants? Because in making pasta, it's the water that's important. And the DelVerde and DeCecco pasta factories are built just a few hundred yards from the headwaters of the Verde River, rushing out of artesian wells deep within the mountains. It's pure, clean mineral water, filtered through the porous rock and selling for the equivalent of a dollar a bottle in restaurants throughout Italy. This clear spring water helps produce a light, delicate pasta which we use exclusively at Castagnola's.

Going to great lengths for the very best ingredients is, in a word, essential. More than anything else, that's the real key to success in cooking Italian.

What makes the world's great chefs great isn't so much their cooking ability as it is their buying ability. A chef scouring the early morning markets in Rome or Naples is a common sight — selecting the best cuts of meat, the freshest fish, the finest vegetables. When he's finished there, the most important part of his job is done. The same holds true for you and me: no matter how careful we are in the kitchen, a meal won't come out right if we didn't shop right first.

The basics are all-important. To ensure that we're using the best possible basic ingredients, Ruth and I have traveled extensively in Italy to visit growers and suppliers personally. Our trips along that narrow mountain road in Fara San Martino were only the beginning.

We've visited the tomato farmers in the San Marzano region, where the world's best plum tomatoes are vine ripened in rich volcanic soil with good drainage. These *pomodori* tomatoes are deep red, meaty and nearly seedless. They're picked by hand, not machine, and taken to processing plants which are all very near the vineyards. They're nice and firm, because they're scalded just enough to loosen and remove the skin, then canned immediately with fresh basil. And because they're low in acid, they produce an exceptionally delicate marinara sauce.

Since 1988, when the U.S. government slapped a 100 percent import tax on such products, San Marzano tomatoes have become too expensive for most restaurateurs. But once again, in the interests of using the very best ingredients, I consider them worth the price. At present, Castagnola's is the only restaurant in Hawaii importing the San Marzano variety.

But the most expensive product isn't always the best product. Consider parmesan cheese, a critical ingredient in many recipes. Conventional wisdom has it that the top-of-the-line parmesan is *parmigiano reggiano*, produced for seven centuries in the tightly controlled Emilia-Romagna zone. I feel, however, that Padano parmesan, from another area of

Italy, actually has a better, more refined flavor. It's certainly the equal of the famous *reggiano*, but like Champagne in France, you can't call it *reggiano* if it's from another region.

When we visited Padano, we saw cows fed a strict diet: no grazing, no consumption of wild plants. And we saw their pure, non-additive cheese squeezed out into wheels and soaked for two weeks in a salt water bath. After that, the wheels are aged for two summers in a warehouse the size of a football stadium, where they're turned and scraped and cleaned every week.

Also in the Parma region, we stopped by the piggeries where hogs are fattened on the rich whey by-product of the parmesan cheese. The result is world-famous Parma ham — a wonderful source of protein and the sweetest, juiciest *prosciutto* you'll ever taste.

And the search goes on. We've driven the back roads of Tuscany to find the people who process the finest extra virgin olive oil. We've toured the water buffalo ranches near Naples, where they make real buffalo mozzarella, and not the cow's milk variety that's usually available these days. We've sampled a smorgasbord of wines at the Bolla winery tasting room. We've checked out the espresso made by the Trieste company that developed its unique pressurization method a half-century ago.

You get the idea. Simply put, the best quality products are worth the effort to find, whether you're on a buying trip through the Italian countryside or stalking the shelves of your neighborhood markets.

In this first chapter, we present some of the basics — breads, flavored extra virgin olive oils, sauces and stocks — made with the best products and useful in many of the recipes to follow.

STOCKS

Beef Stock

- 1 qt. water
- 2 lbs. bones (preferably oxtails or any bone marrow bone)
- 1 tsp. kosher salt
- 1 tsp. pepper
- 1 tblsp. sugar
- 1 oz. or 6 cloves garlic
- 1 medium size yellow onion
- 1 sprig parsley
- 1 stalk celery
- 1 bay leaf (optional)

Brown beef in pot first until sauces stick to the pot. Add water, salt, pepper, sugar, garlic cloves, onion, parsley and celery. Simmer for one to 1½ hours on low heat. Allow to cool. Strain and refrigerate. The next day, remove fat on surface for sauteeing. Use remaining clear broth for soup stock or gravies.

Chicken Stock

- 1 lb. chicken (preferably breast and back area)
- 1 qt. water
- 1 tsp. salt
- 1 tsp. pepper
- 1 oz. or 6 cloves garlic
- ½ medium size yellow onion
- 1 sprig parsley
- 1 stalk celery

Simmer all ingredients on low heat for one hour. Allow to cool. Strain into bowl. Wait till cool, then refrigerate. The next day, remove fat on surface for sauteeing. Use remaining clear broth for soup stock or gravies.

Good soup stock can be a wonderful by-product of other recipes. You can use leftover beef bones or a turkey breast to make a flavorful, natural stock without any chemical additives. I soak pork bones in brine overnight, for example, then smoke them and use them to flavor my bean soup.

Try cooking different meats and poultry together: beef and chicken, veal and pork, turkey and beef or any combination of what you have on hand. The results can be varied and memorable. And you can freeze the stock and use it as needed.

SAUCES

Marinara Sauce

Whenever possible, use canned *pomodori* tomatoes from Italy's San Marzano region, just as we do at Castagnola's. Many other canned tomatoes are labeled "San Marzano-style" or some similar appellation, but your palate will tell you there's no comparison with the real thing.

1 28-oz can Italian tomatoes
1 tblsp. cooked garlic
4 oz. diced onion
3 tblsp. garlic flavored extra virgin olive oil
1 tsp. salt
1 tsp. pepper
1 tsp. sugar
1 tsp. pesto sauce
1 tsp. romano cheese
4 freshly picked sweet Italian basil leaves

In a heavy-bottom sauce pan saute diced onion and olive oil. Add sugar, salt and pepper. When onions are golden brown (but not burned) add cooked garlic, tomatoes and basil. Strain tomatoes first to remove seeds, which can make sauce taste slightly bitter. Simmer, stirring frequently for about 25 minutes. Then add the pesto sauce and romano cheese. Stir and allow to simmer for another 5 minutes.

Pesto Sauce

Pesto means "pounded," and originally, all the ingredients were blended together with a mortar and pestle. These days, of course, your food processor will do a much better job. Remember to use sweet Italian basil and not the Oriental variety, which has a mint flavor.

1 oz. or 6 cloves pure garlic
4 oz. parmesan cheese
4 oz. romano cheese
4 oz. pinole (pine) nuts
2 cups extra virgin olive oil
4 cups clean sweet Italian basil (not pressed tightly)
Pinch of kosher salt

In a blender add basil leaves and olive oil. Add basil to oil while blending slowly. Add garlic and blend until smooth. Add pinole nuts, romano cheese, parmesan cheese and blend until smooth.

FLOUR, CRUMBS AND CROUTONS

Flavored Flour

1 cup flour
1 oz. garlic cloves
1 tsp. kosher salt
1 tsp. dried basil
½ tsp. crushed black pepper

Mix with whisk or in cake mixer for about 15 minutes and set aside in a dry area.

Flavored Bread Crumbs

1 cup bread crumbs
1 oz. or 6 garlic cloves
1 tsp. kosher salt
1 tsp. dried basil
½ tsp. crushed black pepper

Place stale bread in an oven, set on warm, overnight. Grate into bread crumbs. Just as with Flavored Flour, mix in garlic, salt, pepper and oregano for 15 minutes. Let stand.

Flavored Croutons

2 cups 2-day old bread, cubed
¼ cup garlic flavored extra virgin olive oil
1 tsp. kosher salt
1 tsp. dried basil
½ tsp. crushed black pepper

Dry bread on top rack of unheated oven overnight. Cut into cubes. Mix with garlic flavored extra virgin olive oil, salt and pepper and let stand overnight. Bake croutons in oven for one hour at 170 degrees. Makes 1 cup of croutons.

To ensure better accuracy, I try to use weight rather than count or other measuring methods in my recipes. A portion scale is a must in the complete Italian kitchen.

You can store these flavored flours, crumbs and croutons in a cool, dry place and they'll keep for several weeks.

BREAD AND ROLLS

No Italian meal is complete without a crusty, country-style loaf of bread. The higher your oven temperature, the crustier the bread will be on the outside, and the softer it will be inside. Here's where a good dough mixer like the Kitchen Aid comes in handy. It's a whole lot easier than hand mixing and you'll appreciate the difference in the finished product.

In baking bread and rolls, I've found that cake or solid yeast creates a much better finished product than the granulated variety.

1 cup hot water
1 tsp. kosher salt
4 tblsp. honey
1/4 block of block yeast
3 cups unbleached flour

Preheat oven to 400 degrees. Dissolve honey and salt in hot water. Whisk until cooled to baby bottle temperature. Dissolve yeast in mixture until fully cooled. Add $2^{1}/_{2}$ cups of flour, adding the remainder for stiffer dough if necessary. Put dough on counter, cover with warm cloth and let sit for at least 25 minutes, or until doubled in size. Punch down dough and cut into 4 equal parts. Shape into loaves (or 10 equal parts for rolls). Put on baking sheets lined with a little flour or corn meal. Cool. Cover with clean cloth and let rise until double in size. Cut horizontally with sharp knife or razor blade, to allow bread to rise in oven without bursting. Bake 15 minutes for bread and 10 minutes for rolls, turning sheet pan after 8 minutes for even browning. Bread and rolls will be done when it gives off a hollow sound when tapped with a finger. Remove to cooling rack. Makes 4 loaves of bread or 10 rolls.

Top to bottom: giving basil leaves the olfactory test in San Marzano; sampling Valpolicella at the Bolla tasting room in Verona; and meeting with the pomodori *growers in the vineyards of San Marzano. Currently, Castagnola's is the largest importer of Bolla wines in Hawaii.*

In the kitchen of this little restaurant in the Portuguese seaside town of Estoril, I learned some of the secrets of Portuguese cooking. The similarities to Italian cucina *can be striking.*

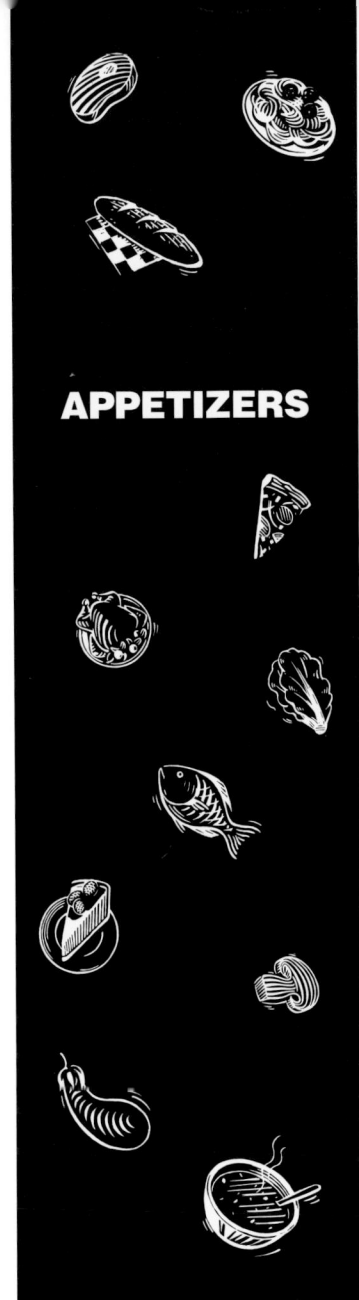

APPETIZERS

Antipasto

As preliminary courses, the recipes on the following pages are probably more American than formal Italian. Several of these can also stand alone as single-course meals, while others can serve as savory condiments and accompaniments to other dishes.

On the following pages, you'll find Sauteed Mushrooms, Shrimp in Butter Sauce, Baked Clams, Cold Eggplant, a terrific Mozzarella and Tomato combination and, of course, a classic Antipasto.

We begin with carpaccio — a big favorite at Castagnola's prepared either hot or cold.

In general, the recipes in this book will serve four people, unless otherwise indicated.

Buon Appetito!

CARPACCIO

Cold carpaccio is an excellent sliced version of steak tartare. The classic Roman carpaccio is served with shavings of truffles and parmesan cheese with a little extra virgin olive oil. However, most chefs in Italy serve it without the truffles for the same reason that we do: the prohibitive cost. At Castagnola's we feature a cold carpaccio with an Oriental twist — sashimi-style with soy sauce and tabasco. The beef is very lean, cut from the scaloppini of the round, which has no gristle or fat whatsoever.

The hot version is known as *bistecca piata grillia* in Italy — beefsteak cooked on the plate. If you don't have a baking stone, simply invert a roasting pan on the bottom of the oven instead. The air inside the pan will distribute the heat evenly across the pan's surface.

Hot Carpaccio

- 4 tblsp. butter
- 4 - 6 oz. top round of beef, thinly sliced
- 1 tsp. Maggi steak sauce
- 8 oz. mushrooms, chopped and sauteed
- 4 tblsp. oregano flavored extra virgin olive oil
- 1 tblsp. freshly ground black pepper
- 1 tsp. kosher salt
- 4 large leaves romaine lettuce, shredded

Preheat oven to 400 degrees. Saute mushrooms. When mushrooms are done, stir in Maggi sauce and butter. Heat and pour over beef as soon as you remove from oven. Spread beef evenly on a baking stone, sizzler or heavy china plate. Brush beef with olive oil. Add pepper and salt. Cook on plate on bottom rack of oven for 4-5 minutes, no more than medium rare. Remove from oven. Top with lettuce and serve immediately with mushroom sauce on sizzling stainless steel plate or china plate placed on insulated liner.

Cold Carpaccio

- 4 oz. very lean top round of beef, thinly sliced
- 1 tblsp. oregano flavored extra virgin olive oil
- 2 tblsp. Maggi steak sauce
- 2 tblsp. soy sauce
- 1/2 tsp. tabasco

Spread beef on plate. Brush with oil. Mix steak sauce, soy sauce and tabasco. Serve beef immediately with sauce mixture in dipping dish on the side.

SPECIALTY BREADS

Garlic Bread

1 loaf French or Italian bread
¼ cup garlic flavored extra virgin olive oil
2 tblsp. presoftened butter mixed with 2 tblsp. cooked chopped garlic and mashed with fork
2 tsp. grated romano cheese
Freshly ground black pepper
Dried oregano

Preheat oven to 350 degrees. Split bread lengthwise down the middle. Brush bread with olive oil. With back of a large spoon, spread butter on bread. Sprinkle with romano cheese, pepper and oregano. Bake in deep baking dish for 15 minutes at 400 degrees. Remove when golden brown. Slice into 2-inch-thick sections. Serve immediately.

Pizza Bread

1 loaf French or Italian bread
4 tblsp. oregano flavored extra virgin olive oil
2 tblsp. grated romano cheese
4 tblsp. marinara pizza sauce (flavored with anchovies)
3 tblsp. shredded mozzarella cheese
1 tsp. dried oregano
1 tsp. fresh ground black pepper

Brush both halves of bread with oil. Top with pizza sauce, romano and mozzarella cheese, oregano and pepper. Bake in baking dish in oven preheated to 400 degrees. Serve whole or cut into 2- to 3-inch slices. If desired, add other pizza toppings such as pepperoni.

ANTIPASTO

This, of course, is the classic Italian starter — a platter of delicate meats, cheeses and vegetables sprinkled with olive oil.

At Castagnola's, we always use Parma *prosciutto*, which has no nitrates or other preservatives. The product wasn't even allowed into this country until a few years ago, when the Italians finally convinced U.S. authorities that their curing methods were just as effective as chemical preservatives.

Parma's sweet, tender ham, which is dried slowly in the region's fresh mountain air, comes from pigs fed the whey by-product of parmesan cheese.

4 slices prosciutto ham
6 slices Genoa salami
4 oz. roasted red peppers, peeled
2 oz. Greek black olives
2 - 4 slices anchovy fillets
2 tomatoes, cut in wedges
5 peppercini peppers
2 tblsp. marinated vegetables
4 oz. fontinella or provolone cheese
4 leaves romaine lettuce
2 tblsp. oregano flavored extra virgin olive oil

Line plate with lettuce. In alternate layers, arrange all ingredients, except oil, on plate. Sprinkle with oil and serve immediately.

SAUTEED MUSHROOMS

1 – 1½ lbs. small button mushrooms
⅛ cup extra virgin olive oil
1 tsp. kosher salt
Freshly ground black pepper

Saute mushrooms in oil. Sprinkle with salt and pepper. Saute 15 minutes over low temperature. Serve immediately. Serves 4 - 6.

While we prefer the small button mushrooms here, you can substitute other varieties. Try to cook all vegetables in a cast iron skillet. It will improve the flavor and add extra iron to your diet, too!

GARLIC BUTTER SPREAD

½ cup extra virgin olive oil
½ lb. softened butter
4 oz. peeled garlic, chopped fine
½ tsp. kosher salt

Blend butter, garlic and salt until paste forms. Turn off blender. Add olive oil to remove the butter from blades. Blend and place in a covered bowl. This will keep refrigerated for at least a week.

This garlic butter spread works wonders when making garlic bread, flavoring sauces or bread crumbs or creating crusty topping for clam, chicken or fish dishes.

FRESH MOZZARELLA AND TOMATO SALAD

The very best mozzarella is buffalo mozzarella, particularly from the pampered water buffalo grazing just east of Naples. Originally, mozzarella was produced almost exclusively from buffalo milk; today it's made mostly from cow's milk. So be selective and make sure you buy the best — real "boofalo" mozzarella from Naples.

5 oz. mozzarella cheese, sliced as thinly as possible
1 tomato, sliced to same thinness
Fresh basil leaves
1 heaping tblsp. pesto sauce
2 tblsp. oregano flavored extra virgin olive oil

Arrange cheese and tomatoes on plate alternately. Decorate with basil leaves. Place pesto sauce in center of plate. Sprinkle oil over top and serve with peppermill.

COLD EGGPLANT

- 1 large round American eggplant, peeled and sliced lengthwise
- 1 tblsp. kosher salt
- 1 cup marinara sauce
- 1/4 cup hot pepper flavored extra virgin olive oil
- 1/4 cup flavored bread crumbs
- 1 egg
- 1/4 cup romano cheese
- Lettuce
- Black olives
- Pimiento

Preheat oven to 325 degrees. Sprinkle eggplant with salt, put in a layer, and let sit for 25 minutes. Press juice out, rinse with water, press again and pat dry. Dip eggplant in egg and flavored bread crumbs. Saute eggplant in oil. Remove from pan and place in baking dish, layering slices with marinara sauce and romano. Set baking dish in larger baking pan with water up to eggplant level to keep the edges from scorching during baking. Bake 1/2 hour until sauce bubbles. Cool on cooling rack. Refrigerate. Slice and serve on bed of lettuce, garnished with black olives and pimiento.

FRESH MOZZARELLA AND TOMATO SALAD

The very best mozzarella is buffalo mozzarella, particularly from the pampered water buffalo grazing just east of Naples. Originally, mozzarella was produced almost exclusively from buffalo milk; today it's made mostly from cow's milk. So be selective and make sure you buy the best — real "boofalo" mozzarella from Naples.

5 oz. mozzarella cheese, sliced as thinly as possible
1 tomato, sliced to same thinness
Fresh basil leaves
1 heaping tblsp. pesto sauce
2 tblsp. oregano flavored extra virgin olive oil

Arrange cheese and tomatoes on plate alternately. Decorate with basil leaves. Place pesto sauce in center of plate. Sprinkle oil over top and serve with peppermill.

SHRIMP AND SPICY BUTTER SAUCE

1 lb. shrimp
1/4 cup garlic flavored extra virgin olive oil
1 tblsp. paprika
1 tblsp. butter
1 tsp. cayenne pepper
1 tsp. kosher salt

In a cast iron skillet, saute whole shrimp in oil for 5 minutes, until shrimp turn pink. Mix in paprika, cayenne and salt. Add butter. Shut off heat. Arrange shrimp on plate in a circle with small chafing dish or cup in the center. Pour pan juices in center for dipping. Serve with lemon wedges and a finger bowl.

BAKED CLAMS AREGINATA

Areginata has nothing to do with oregano, though many people confuse the two. At Castagnola's our fresh clams arrive every Wednesday morning from the West Coast. The Pacific Ocean salt content there is one cup of kosher salt to two gallons of water. We always purge the clams in the same mixture to eliminate the slight iodine taste from kelp and algae. This salt water bath ensures a sweeter taste. Try it.

2 dozen clams
Juice of 1 lemon
1/4 cup flavored bread crumbs
1 tblsp. romano cheese
4 tblsp. oregano flavored extra virgin olive oil
4 oz. butter

Preheat oven to 400 degrees. Open clams and strain the broth in a bowl. Mix broth with bread crumbs, add oil, lemon juice and romano. Mix to a paste consistency. Spoon mixture on top of each open clam shell. Sprinkle with remaining oil and butter. Bake until golden brown. Garnish with wheels of lemon and fresh parsley. Serve immediately.

COLD EGGPLANT

- 1 large round American eggplant, peeled and sliced lengthwise
- 1 tblsp. kosher salt
- 1 cup marinara sauce
- 1/4 cup hot pepper flavored extra virgin olive oil
- 1/4 cup flavored bread crumbs
- 1 egg
- 1/4 cup romano cheese
- Lettuce
- Black olives
- Pimiento

Preheat oven to 325 degrees. Sprinkle eggplant with salt, put in a layer, and let sit for 25 minutes. Press juice out, rinse with water, press again and pat dry. Dip eggplant in egg and flavored bread crumbs. Saute eggplant in oil. Remove from pan and place in baking dish, layering slices with marinara sauce and romano. Set baking dish in larger baking pan with water up to eggplant level to keep the edges from scorching during baking. Bake 1/2 hour until sauce bubbles. Cool on cooling rack. Refrigerate. Slice and serve on bed of lettuce, garnished with black olives and pimiento.

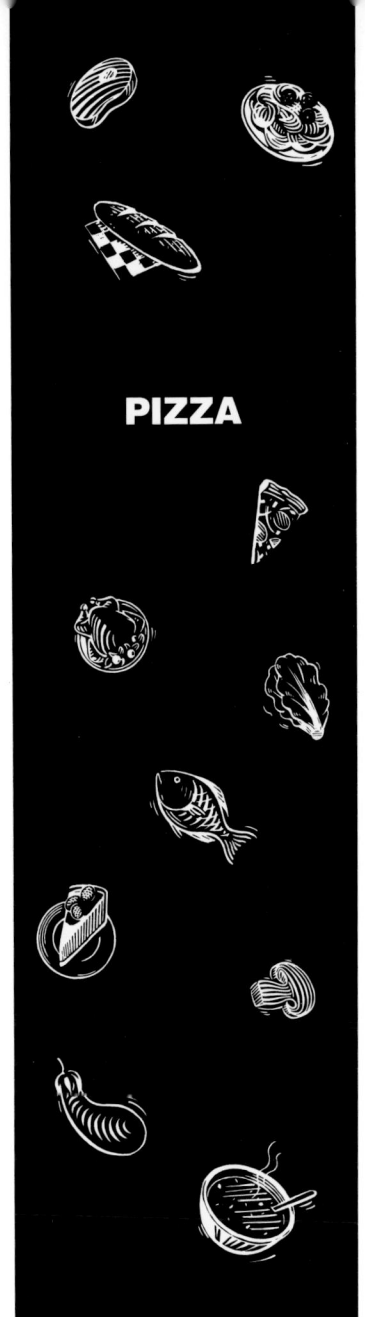

This all-American favorite got its start in the back streets of Naples. Many years ago, the story goes — when the area was ruled by Greece — Neapolitan cooks began piling their ingredients on Greek pita bread. Like pita, the dough was simply shaped and popped right into the oven without being allowed to rise. Pita became pizza, and the rest is culinary history.

Today's American pizza is a much more exciting version of the comparably bland Italian pizza, which is often just tomatoes on pita bread with a little mozzarella. At Castagnola's, we make New York-style pizza, adding more Romano cheese to give it some extra kick.

The pros use a pizza stone to distribute the heat evenly beneath the pizza. While it's nice to have one of these, there's a simple alternative. Invert a large roasting pan in the oven and preheat for at least 25 minutes. Then place an aluminum pizza pan on top of that. The hot air under the roasting pan provides the same even distribution of heat.

One caveat: keep the number of toppings to a dull roar — preferably no more than two plus the cheese. Too many will add excessive moisture and leave you with a soggy pizza. This is especially true of vegetables. Also, unless you like raw vegetable pizza, pre-cook veggies before you add them as a topping.

There's one other big difference between Italian and American pizza, by the way. Italians don't eat it with their hands!

PIZZA

Pizza sauce differs from basic marinara sauce in that anchovies are finely chopped and blended in. In this way, the anchovies bring out the flavor rather than overpowering the sauce. Add one anchovy fillet for a single pizza and let the sauce stand in the refrigerator overnight.

Brush the crust of the dough with olive oil only where the tomato sauce will be. This will keep the sauce from penetrating the dough and creating a soggy pizza. Don't brush the edge of the loaf, however; the dough will rise better without it.

12 oz. pizza dough
1 cup marinara sauce
2 anchovy fillets
1 tsp. dried oregano
Grated romano cheese
Grated mozzarella cheese
Oregano flavored extra virgin olive oil

Preheat oven to 450 degrees.

For pizza crust: Use same recipe as bread dough, reducing honey to 1 tblsp. Cut dough into sections and roll out on flour. Shape into pizza pan brushed lightly with oregano flavored extra virgin olive oil. Brush center of crust with oregano flavored extra virgin olive oil.

For sauce: In blender, mix marinara sauce, anchovy fillets and oregano. Spread sauce on pizza crust. Top with cheeses and any other topping of your choice. Bake 15 minutes on bottom shelf of oven, on baking stone or large roasting pan inverted on bottom shelf. Rotate occasionally to ensure even baking.

CALZONE

2½ – 3 oz. pizza dough
2 tblsp. ricotta cheese
1 tblsp. romano cheese
Mushrooms, prosciutto, pepperoni (optional)

Roll dough (see page 33) into 9-inch circle. Place filling on center of dough and fold over end to end apple turnover-style. Seal edges with water or egg wash. Use fork to poke three holes into calzone. Deep fry or brush with oregano flavored extra virgin olive oil and bake 15 minutes in 400-degree oven, turning halfway. Serve hot.

POCKET PIZZA

We have the Big Mac people to thank for this one. When McDonald's held its national sales meeting at the Kahala Hilton in Honolulu, they asked me to make a test calzone for possible addition to their fast-food menu. "Where's the tomato sauce?" they asked when I brought it in. "Calzone doesn't have tomato sauce," I said. "What you really want is a pocket pizza." So I created one for them that we all loved. McDonald's hasn't made it available yet, but Castagnola's certainly has!

2 1/2 - 3 oz. Pizza dough
1 tblsp. oregano flavored extra virgin olive oil
1 tblsp. pizza sauce
1 tblsp. romano cheese
1 tblsp. mozzarella cheese, grated or chopped fine

Roll dough into 9-inch round. Brush with oregano flavored extra virgin olive oil. Add pizza sauce, cheeses and other optional toppings. Fold over center and seal with a fork and egg wash, calzone-style. Poke with fork holes. Deep fry, or brush with extra virgin olive oil and bake, 15 minutes in 400-degree oven.

PREFERRED PASTA

Here are some of the most popular kinds of pasta we use at Castagnola's. Clockwise from right: mezzi tubetti, angel hair pasta, penne (cut at an angle like a quill, or pen), lasagne doppia riccia, rigatoni, tagliatelle and linguine.

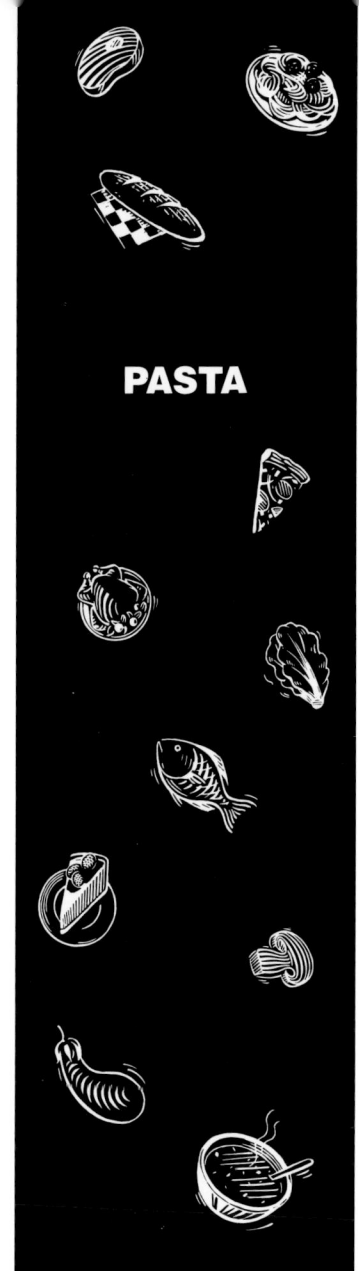

Fettucine Mia Figlia

The way some people tell it, Italians were strangers to pasta until Marco Polo went to China. But the fact is, it was round noodles that Polo discovered there. There already were plenty of the flat variety, like fettucine and linguine. So yes, he learned to make round spaghetti in China; and no, he didn't learn the art of pasta.

And "art" it is — a simple yet versatile staple which can make or break an Italian meal. The art of pasta making involves the right water, the right flour and the right techniques. At Castagnola's, we use the light, delicate pasta from the DelVerde plant in Abruzzi, Italy. It's a long way to go for pasta, but getting the best makes it worth the trip.

While the following recipes can be served with just about any pasta, there are also some good reasons behind the combinations here. We serve Linguine Aglia Olio, for instance, because the fine grain of the linguine will absorb the flavor of the *aglia olio* sauce better than, say, the heavier rigatoni.

Still, because part of the fun is in the experimentation, any dish here can be created with your choice of pasta.

CHICKEN LINGUINE

- 1 lb. fresh chicken, julienned
- 1 carrot, peeled and julienned
- 1 lb. linguine
- 1 green bell pepper, seeded and julienned
- 1 red bell pepper, seeded and julienned
- 1/2 zucchini squash, julienned (leave skin on)
- 1/2 lb. sliced mushrooms
- Kosher salt
- Freshly ground black pepper
- 1 tblsp. dried basil
- 2 tsp. romano cheese
- 4 tblsp. garlic flavored extra virgin olive oil

Saute chicken 5-10 minutes in garlic flavored extra virgin olive oil. Add carrots and saute 4-5 minutes. Add peppers, zucchini and mushrooms. Sprinkle with salt, pepper and basil. Cook linguine in 2 qts. boiling water. Toss cooked linguine in pan with chicken and vegetables. Sprinkle with romano cheese and serve immediately.

LINGUINE PESTO

2 qts. water
1 lb. linguine
1 tsp. kosher salt
2 tblsp. pesto sauce
Fresh basil
Romano cheese
1/4 cup pasta water

Bring water to boil in saucepan. Add salt. Break linguine in half and place in water, tossing continually for 4 - 5 minutes until al dente. Strain linguine, retaining 1/4 cup of the pasta water. In a cast iron skillet mix pesto sauce and pasta water. Bring to simmer. Place linguine on plate. Pour sauce over pasta. Top with 1 tblsp. pesto sauce in center. Garnish with basil, sprinkle with cheese and serve immediately.

You've noticed that many cooks rinse their pasta after cooking. Don't do it! Rinsing removes both flavor and nutritional value. At Castagnola's, we never, ever rinse our pasta!

LINGUINE MARINARA

Marinara was named after sailors — not seafood, as is the popular misconception. Originally, this simple dish was whipped up for sailors in port, who were often in a hurry to be somewhere else.

This tomato sauce is a most basic Italian recipe. You can *add* seafood, of course. You can add raw peppers and anchovies to create a putanesca sauce. You can add bacon and hot peppers and make arrabiata. Marinara, in fact, can provide the base for many Italian sauces. Here it's presented in its simple form over linguine.

2 qts. water
1 tsp. kosher salt
1 lb. linguine
1 cup marinara sauce
Fresh basil
Grated romano cheese

Bring water to a boil. Add salt. Add linguine, broken in half. Simmer for 5 minutes. Strain linguine and place on plate. Pour marinara sauce over top. Garnish with basil and cheese.

LINGUINE TUTTO GIARDINO

- 3 tblsp. garlic flavored extra virgin olive oil
- 1 large carrot, peeled and julienned
- 1 zucchini, julienned
- 1/2 lb. mushrooms, sliced
- 1 red pepper, seeded and julienned
- 1 green pepper, seeded and julienned
- 2 slices of eggplant, julienned, salted and wrung out
- 1/2 medium yellow onion
- 2 qts. water
- 1 tsp. kosher salt
- 1 lb. linguine
- Romano cheese

In a cast iron skillet, saute in oil the carrot, mushrooms, peppers, onion and eggplant. Bring water and salt to boil. Break linguine in half and cook 4 - 5 minutes until al dente. Drain pasta, leaving it a little wet. Toss pasta into skillet with vegetables. Serve immediately, sprinkled with romano cheese. Garnish with basil and parsley.

This one is almost a zero cholesterol dish. It translates as "the total garden" and can incorporate just about any vegetable you'd like. Just be sure to cut the vegetables according to the shape of the pasta. Here, for instance, you julienne them to complement the linguine. If you opt for Rigatoni Tutto Giardino, you should dice the vegetables to match that pasta.

LINGUINE PRIMAVERA

Primavera means springtime, and this recipe calls only for the earlier spring vegetables such as carrots and zucchini. It differs from the Linguine Tutto Giardino on the opposite page primarily in that it calls for a creamier, cheesier sauce.

2 qts. water
1 lb. linguine
1/4 cup garlic flavored extra virgin olive oil
1 large carrot, peeled and julienned
1 large zucchini, julienned
1/2 lb. fresh mushrooms, sliced
1 red pepper, seeded and julienned
1 green pepper, seeded and julienned
2 tsp. kosher salt
Freshly ground black pepper
1 tsp. dried basil
1 egg yolk
2 tblsp. butter
1 tsp. romano cheese

In a cast iron skillet saute in oil the carrot, mushrooms, peppers and zucchini. Sprinkle with 1 tsp. salt, pepper and basil. In a stainless steel bowl, melt butter. Add egg yolk and romano. Whip together and set aside, keeping it warm. Bring water to boil. Add 1 tsp. salt. Break linguine in half and add to water. Cook for 4-5 minutes, stirring continuously. Drain, leaving a little bit of water dripping off the pasta. Toss immediately in bowl with butter mixture. Add sauteed vegetables. Toss and serve immediately, garnished with fresh parsley or basil.

RIGATONI RICOTTA

2 qts. water
1 tsp. kosher salt
1 lb. rigatoni
1/4 lb. ricotta cheese
2 tblsp. romano cheese
1 cup marinara sauce

Boil water. Add salt then rigatoni and cook 12 minutes. In a saucepan, slowly heat marinara sauce. Place ricotta and romano in a heated bowl until softened. Drain rigatoni well, add to heated bowl. Toss with cheeses. Serve, topped with marinara sauce and a sprinkling of romano cheese and 1 tablespoon riccota on top. Garnish with 3 fresh basil leaves.

LINGUINE PRIMAVERA

Primavera means springtime, and this recipe calls only for the earlier spring vegetables such as carrots and zucchini. It differs from the Linguine Tutto Giardino on the opposite page primarily in that it calls for a creamier, cheesier sauce.

2 qts. water
1 lb. linguine
1/4 cup garlic flavored extra virgin olive oil
1 large carrot, peeled and julienned
1 large zucchini, julienned
1/2 lb. fresh mushrooms, sliced
1 red pepper, seeded and julienned
1 green pepper, seeded and julienned
2 tsp. kosher salt
Freshly ground black pepper
1 tsp. dried basil
1 egg yolk
2 tblsp. butter
1 tsp. romano cheese

In a cast iron skillet saute in oil the carrot, mushrooms, peppers and zucchini. Sprinkle with 1 tsp. salt, pepper and basil. In a stainless steel bowl, melt butter. Add egg yolk and romano. Whip together and set aside, keeping it warm. Bring water to boil. Add 1 tsp. salt. Break linguine in half and add to water. Cook for 4-5 minutes, stirring continuously. Drain, leaving a little bit of water dripping off the pasta. Toss immediately in bowl with butter mixture. Add sauteed vegetables. Toss and serve immediately, garnished with fresh parsley or basil.

LINGUINE AGLIO OLIO

½ cup garlic flavored extra virgin olive oil
2 anchovy fillets
3 tblsp. cooked garlic
2 qts. water
1 tsp. kosher salt
1 lb. linguine
Romano cheese
Fresh basil

In a cast iron skillet, heat oil. Crush anchovy fillets into oil with a fork. Add garlic. Bring water and salt to boil. Break linguine in half and add to water. Stir and cook continuously 4 - 5 minutes until al dente. Drain and toss with anchovy/oil mixture. Sprinkle with cheese and serve garnished with fresh basil.

When traveling through Italy, I'm always struck by the variation in *aglio olio* sauces — some fairly flat and bland, others considerably tastier. The difference is in the anchovies. When cooking with anchovies, crush them with a fork in warm — not hot — olive oil to perk up the flavor. The same holds true in making Caesar salad dressing or pizza sauce. Even those who turn up their noses at anchovies can appreciate the difference.

LINGUINE WITH CLAM SAUCE

For red clam sauce, simply substitute marinara sauce for the wine. For green sauce, use pesto sauce.

If no fresh clams are available, you can use a 10-ounce can of chopped clams.

- 2 tblsp. garlic flavored extra virgin olive oil
- 2 tblsp. Italian white wine
- 1 tblsp. dried basil
- 2 dozen small fresh clams
- 2 qts. water
- 1 tsp. kosher salt
- 1 lb. linguine

In saucepan, place oil, wine and basil. Bring to high heat. Add clams. Cover with tight lid and steam for 5-10 minutes, until all clams are open. Bring water and salt to boil. Break linguine in half and add to water. Stir and cook continuously 4 - 5 minutes until al dente. Place on a platter topped with clams and sauce. Garnish with basil.

RIGATONI RICOTTA

- 2 qts. water
- 1 tsp. kosher salt
- 1 lb. rigatoni
- 1/4 lb. ricotta cheese
- 2 tblsp. romano cheese
- 1 cup marinara sauce

Boil water. Add salt then rigatoni and cook 12 minutes. In a saucepan, slowly heat marinara sauce. Place ricotta and romano in a heated bowl until softened. Drain rigatoni well, add to heated bowl. Toss with cheeses. Serve, topped with marinara sauce and a sprinkling of romano cheese and 1 tablespoon riccota on top. Garnish with 3 fresh basil leaves.

RIGATONI ARRABIATA

This one is my favorite pasta. *Arrabiata* means raging, as in *spicy*. If the hot peppers don't agree with you, you can eliminate them. But don't forget: eating spicy food is just like good aerobic exercise. It can make the blood race and bring your resting heart rate down. And all without damaging your knees or your arches! That's why researchers have found some of the lowest heart failure rates in the country along the Tex-Mex border — a real hotbed of spicy food.

- 2 qts. water
- 1 tsp. kosher salt
- 1 lb. rigatoni
- 4 slices of bacon, diced
- 1 tsp. crushed red pepper (optional)
- 1/2 cup marinara sauce
- 1 tsp. dried basil
- 1 tblsp. romano cheese
- 1/4 cup garlic flavored extra virgin olive oil

Bring water to boil and add salt. Add rigatoni and cook 12 minutes. In a cast iron skillet, saute bacon and pepper over low temperature until bacon is soft. Add marinara sauce and basil. Simmer slowly. Drain rigatoni well. Place rigatoni in heated bowl; toss with romano and oil. Top with bacon/marinara sauce. Serve with grated romano cheese.

FETTUCINE CASTAGNOLA

2 qts. water
1 tsp. kosher salt
1 lb. egg noodle fettucine
1/2 lb. sliced mushrooms
2 tblsp. butter
2 tblsp. romano cheese
1 egg yolk
Parmesan cheese
Fresh parsley

Bring water to boil. Add salt. Cook fettucine in water 6 - 8 minutes until al dente. Saute mushrooms and set aside. In a heated bowl, add butter until it melts. Whip in egg yolk until it froths. Add romano and mushrooms. Drain fettucine, not well, with water still dripping. Toss immediately in heated bowl with egg mixture. Serve immediately on heated plates with a sprinkling of parmesan cheese. Garnish with fresh parsley.

This menu item was prompted by regional differences over Fettucine Alfredo. In Italy and on the East Coast, there's no cream in that dish, while the West Coast version has plenty of it.

So pay attention now: Fettucine Castagnola is actually East Coast Alfredo, with eggs, butter and cheese — and no cream. But when we actually *call* it Alfredo, all the Californians cry, "Hey! *This* ain't Fettucine Alfredo!"

At Castagnola's, we aim to please.

FETTUCINE CARBONARA

Carbonara works best with a long thin pasta to hold the sauce. I like an egg noodle fettucine for that purpose. My wife, Ruth, prefers linguine. In Italy, both Linguine Carbonara and Spaghetti Carbonara are more popular. Try some substitutions and decide for yourself.

2 qts. water
1 tsp. kosher salt
1 lb. egg noodle fettucine
4 slices bacon, diced
1 medium yellow onion, diced
3 tblsp. garlic flavored extra virgin olive oil
1/4 cup imported Italian white wine
2 tblsp. butter
Freshly ground black pepper
3 tblsp. romano cheese
Fresh American or Italian parsley

Boil water and add salt. Mix in pasta and cook 6 to 8 minutes until al dente. While pasta is cooking, in a heavy saucepan saute bacon and onion in the oil. Cook bacon until clear, not browned. Add wine and cook down. Add butter. Drain pasta, leaving pasta very wet, mix with 2 tsp. butter and romano cheese and place on plates. Spoon sauce over top of pasta. Serve garnished with sprigs of parsley.

FETTUCINE MIA FIGLIA

When my daughter, Barbara, visited us from New Jersey recently, she brought along an excellent fettucine recipe. I liked it so much that I immediately added it to the Castagnola's menu and named it Fettucine Mia Figlia, "my daughter's fettucine."

2 qts. water
1 lb. egg noodle fettucine
1 large garlic clove per serving
Handful fresh basil chopped coarsely per serving
2 tblsp. marscapone cheese per serving (or good cream cheese)
2 tblsp. milk
Light salt
Freshly ground white pepper

Saute finely chopped garlic and basil in olive oil. When garlic is golden, lower the heat and spoon in the marscapone, salt, pepper and milk. Toss with freshly cooked fettucine. Sprinkle 1/2 tsp. romano per serving. Toss well, garnish with fresh basil and serve.

BAKED ZITI

1 lb. ziti
2 qts. water
1 tsp. kosher salt
1 tblsp. extra virgin olive oil
3 cups milk
4 tblsp. butter
4 tblsp. herb flour
Generous amount of freshly ground black pepper
1 cup marinara sauce
$1 1/3$ cups romano cheese
$1 1/3$ cups parmesan cheese, grated
$1 1/3$ cups mozzarella cheese

Preheat oven to 325 degrees. In a heavy saucepan boil water and salt. Add ziti and cook very al dente. Drain immediately, rinse with cold water and mix with oil to prevent pasta from sticking together. Set aside. In the same saucepan, melt butter over low heat. Stir in flour. Add milk slowly, stirring. Add 1 cup each romano and parmesan cheese, heat just below boiling, until cheese is dissolved. Stir in ziti. In baking dish brushed with olive oil, place ziti and top with marinara sauce spread out evenly. Top with mozzarella and remaining romano and parmesan. Bake 25 to 35 minutes, until ziti is bubbling. Serve within $1/2$ hour.

NOTE: Penne or elbow macaroni may be used instead of ziti.

This is the traditional pasta dish served at formal Italian weddings; some even call it bridegroom's pasta. It's also served often on Fridays in Italy, because it contains no meat. In that respect, you might say it's the Italian equivalent of good old American-style macaroni and cheese. You can make it the night before and just bake before serving.

Ziti should be slightly crunchy when served, and that's what you get when it's baked in the cheese and marinara sauce. Otherwise, the end result is mushy or, as the Italians say, *svatta*.

POULTRY

Gone are the days when you could visit the local poultry market, select a live chicken, then wait while they butchered it for you right on the spot. These days, you can't be sure it's quite that fresh.

So find out when your market receives its chicken deliveries. If you shop on Monday, for example, you might get "fresh" chicken that's been refrigerated since Friday. Go later in the week instead.

Most of a chicken's flavor is in the skin and at Castagnola's, we always serve it with skin intact. If you're cholesterol conscious, it's still better to cook it that way and remove the skin before serving. With this method, any traces of cholesterol are negligible.

And on that score: cook with chicken fat whenever possible. It has about half the cholesterol of butter and it enhances flavor, too.

CHICKEN SICILIANO

- 2 lbs. boneless fresh chicken, cut in 2-inch slices
- 1/2 cup herb flour for dredging
- 1/4 cup garlic flavored extra virgin olive oil
- 4 large potatoes, peeled and cut in eighths
- 1 tsp. kosher salt
- Freshly ground black pepper
- 1/8 tsp. powdered thyme
- 1 tblsp. oregano
- 1 medium yellow onion, peeled and quartered
- 1 green bell pepper, julienned and seeded
- 1 red bell pepper, julienned and seeded
- 1/2 lb. mushrooms, sliced
- 4 Greek olives, pitted
- 1/4 cup Italian white wine
- 1/4 cup chicken stock
- Tomato wedges
- Parsley

In a cast iron skillet, simmer potatoes in oil for 20 minutes at low heat, covered. Add salt, pepper and thyme. Add onions and simmer 10 minutes. Dredge chicken in flour. Add chicken, saute 10 minutes on each side then add peppers, mushroom and olives. Simmer 10-15 minutes. Add wine and cook down. Add stock. Simmer 5 minutes. Serve garnished with tomato wedges and parsley.

CHICKEN ARRICCIATA

- 1- 1½ lbs. fresh boneless chicken cut in 2-inch slices
- 1 cup herb flour
- 1 large head escarole (or romaine), broken into large pieces
- ¼ cup garlic flavored extra virgin olive oil
- ½ tsp. dry crushed red pepper (optional)
- 1 tsp. kosher salt
- Freshly ground black pepper
- 1 tsp. dried basil
- 1 lb. egg noodle fettucine
- ¼ cup Italian white wine

Boil 2 qts. water. Dredge chicken in flour. In a cast iron skillet, saute chicken in oil for 10 minutes. Add red pepper, salt, black pepper and basil. Put fettucine in boiling water. Turn chicken and simmer 10 minutes. Add chopped escarole and wine; cover with tight lid and simmer 5 minutes. Drain fettucine; toss in bowl with a little olive oil. Place fettucine on plates and spoon chicken on top.

CHICKEN CACCIATORE

Cacciatore means "hunter" and this dish is traditionally served hunter-style — outdoors in a big pot. Seems as if every country in Europe has its own version; in France, for instance, it's called *poulet chaisseur.*

When you think about it, this kind of cross-cultural borrowing is common. My Chicken Vegetable Linguine was directly inspired by chicken chow mein, while ravioli is nothing more than Italian won ton!

- 2 lbs. fresh boneless chicken, sliced in 2-inch-wide diagonals
- 1/2 cup herb flour for dredging
- 1 cup garlic flavored extra virgin olive oil
- 1 red bell pepper, seeded and julienned
- 1 green bell pepper, seeded and julienned
- 1/4 lb. mushrooms, sliced
- 4 Greek olives, pitted
- 1/4 cup Italian red wine
- 1 tsp. kosher salt
- Freshly ground black pepper
- 1 tblsp. dried basil
- 1/2 cup marinara sauce

Dredge chicken in flour. In a cast iron skillet saute chicken in oil for 5 minutes. Add peppers and mushrooms. Simmer 5 minutes. Add olives and simmer 5 minutes. Add red wine and simmer until wine cooks down completely. Add 1 cup marinara sauce and simmer 5 minutes. Serve with your choice of pasta on the side or — if you're counting calories — with a salad.

CHICKEN PAPRIKA

5 red bell peppers, seeded and julienned
¼ cup garlic flavored extra virgin olive oil
1½ – 2 lbs. fresh boneless chicken cut into 2-inch-wide strips
½ cup herb flour for dredging
2 tblsp. paprika
Pinch of cayenne pepper (optional)
4 tblsp. butter

In heavy saucepan, saute peppers in oil, 5 to 15 minutes. Remove peppers from pan and set aside. Dredge chicken slices in herb flour and saute in saucepan, 5 minutes per side. Sprinkle chicken with paprika (and cayenne). Simmer 5 minutes. Add peppers to pan, cover tightly and simmer 10-20 minutes. Serve immediately.

CHICKEN PORTUGUESE

There are many similarities between Italian and Portuguese cooking. Some of the secrets of the latter were revealed to me at a wonderful little restaurant in the Portuguese seaside town of Estoril. Like Italians, the Portuguese produce excellent olive oil and use it as a cooking base. But they season dishes with coriander instead of basil and oregano, and they pre-flavor their oil with Portuguese sausage and sweet red peppers.

The recipe here can also be used with beef or pork. Suggestion: serve Chicken Portuguese with Potatoes Castagnola.

- 2 lbs. fresh boneless chicken, cut in 2-inch slices
- 1/2 cup herb flour
- 1/8 cup garlic flavored extra virgin olive oil
- 2 red bell peppers, seeded and julienned
- 4 - 6 Greek olives, pitted
- 1/2 cup Italian white wine
- 1 cup chicken stock
- 1 tblsp. coriander powder
- 2 oz. thin-sliced Portuguese sausage or pepperoni

Dredge chicken in flour. Saute pepper and sausage 5 minutes. Add olives. Saute 5 minutes more. Remove and save. Add chicken, brown on both sides 10-15 minutes; add wine and cook down. Add peppers, sausage, olives, coriander and stock and simmer 10 minutes.

CHICKEN AREGINATA

- 1½ – 2 lbs. boneless chicken (thighs or breasts) pounded to make cutlets, leave skin on
- ½ cup herb flour for dredging
- ½ cup garlic flavored extra virgin olive oil
- ½ cup Areginata Paste

Preheat oven to 400 degrees. Preheat cast iron skillet or heavy bottomed sauce pan with half of the oil.

Dredge chicken cutlets in herb flour. Saute on medium heat, skin side up, for 5 minutes. Place chicken skin side down in sheet pan brushed with olive oil. Spread top with Areginata Paste, about ⅛ inch. Place in oven. Bake 20-25 minutes until crust browns on top. Garnish with lemon wedges and parsley.

Areginata Paste

- 1 cup flavored bread crumbs
- 2 tblsp. garlic butter
- 4 tblsp. oregano flavored extra virgin olive oil
- 1 tblsp. dried oregano
- Juice of 1½ lemons
- 2-3 tblsp. beer

Mix all ingredients together, using beer to bring to paste consistency.

Hawaii's clear, warm waters are teeming with some of the best-eating fish in the world. From rich fishing grounds like Penguin Banks near west Molokai and the waters off the Kona Coast and leeward Oahu, island skippers bring back a bounty of ono, mahimahi, yellowfin tuna, Pacific blue marlin and snapper of every stripe. All of which gives Hawaii's cooks an excellent choice of fresh fish.

At Castagnola's, the fish of choice is usually — though certainly not always — ono, or wahoo. This delicious whitefish is firm, tender and a customer favorite. But if good, fresh whitefish isn't available where you live, swordfish, tuna and striped bass can make fine substitutes.

If at all possible, shop for fish at a fish market, not a supermarket. Most important, use your nose. Fish should smell fresh — like the ocean. Sounds obvious, I know, but too many shoppers ignore that critical olfactory test. Look for nice pink gills and clear eyes, too, since that's where fish first begins to deteriorate.

Of course, the best way to find fresh fish is to meet the sportfishing boats on arrival at the dock. You probably won't save any money, but you'll know it's fresh!

MIXED SEAFOOD JAMBALAYA

Jambalaya in an Italian cookbook? What makes this one fit for a *paisan* is that it's served in linguine rather than the Creole-style rice. At Castagnola's, our customers tell us they prefer the linguine for its lightness. The name of the dish, incidentally, comes from the French word for ham, *jambon*.

- 1 lb. linguine
- 2 qts. water
- 1 tsp. kosher salt
- 1 lb. fresh boneless chicken, cut diagonally in 2-inch slices
- 1/4 cup garlic flavored extra virgin olive oil
- 4 1/8- inch slices of Italian ham, diced
- 1 cup chicken stock
- 1 cup marinara sauce
- 1/4 cup Italian white wine
- 1 tsp. kosher salt
- Freshly ground black pepper
- 1 tsp. hot pepper (optional)
- 1 doz. whole white clams
- 1 doz. large shrimp, deveined
- 2 tblsp. romano cheese

Bring water to boil, add salt and cook pasta 4 to 5 minutes. Cook chicken in oil 10 minutes. Add shrimp, salt and pepper. Cook 5 minutes. Add wine, stock, marinara sauce and ham. When mixture comes to a boil, add clams. Cover pan with tight lid and cook 5 to 10 minutes until clams all steam open. Remove lid and continue simmering until mixture thickens. Drain pasta well and toss in bowl with romano cheese. Serve on plates and cover with seafood mixture. Garnish with lemon wheels and fresh parsley.

CALAMARI SCAMPI

4 calamari steaks, pounded thin
¼ cup herb flour
¼ cup garlic flavored extra virgin olive oil
¼ cup Italian white wine
4 tblsp. diced cooked garlic
2 tblsp. butter
2 tblsp. romano cheese

Dredge calamari steaks in herb flour. Saute in oil 5 minutes per side. Add wine. Remove calamari. Add butter and garlic and simmer. Pour over calamari steaks. Sprinkle with romano cheese.

FISH WITH BUTTER AND PAPRIKA

1½ – 2 lbs. fresh fish (ono, mahimahi, Hawaiian cod, halibut)
1 cup herb flour for dredging
¼ lb. butter
¼ cup garlic flavored extra virgin olive oil
Salt and pepper to taste
1 tblsp. paprika

Carefully remove all bones from fish. Cut in 2- to 3-inch slices. Dredge in herb flour. Preheat cast iron skillet or heavy bottomed pan. Add oil; when heated, add fish. Saute on medium heat, 5 minutes. Turn and sprinkle fish with salt, pepper and paprika. Simmer 4 minutes. Add butter. When butter melts, remove fish to serving platter. Give pan juices a quick stir and pour over fish. Garnish with lemon wedges.

BEER BATTER FRIED FISH

In making batter for deep frying, always use beer rather than water. You'll find your batter considerably lighter and fluffier. It's important to let the beer and flour mixture stand overnight to allow fermentation. This beer batter, by the way, is great for onion rings, too.

Your fryer oil can be strained through cheesecloth and used again.

2 1/2 lbs. fresh ono or mahimahi cut in 2-inch strips
1 cup flour
1 cup beer
1 egg yolk
1 tsp. baking powder
1 tsp. kosher salt
Fresh ground black pepper

Fill fryer with garlic flavored extra virgin olive oil, 1 inch deep. Mix 1/2 cup flour with beer and let stand overnight. The next day, add 1/2 cup flour, egg yolk, baking powder, salt and pepper. Stir in well. Wash and drain fish well. Pat dry with paper towel. Dip fish one or two pieces at a time in the batter and immediately place in fryer until fish floats on top and appears golden brown. Turn once and fry for another 5 minutes, then remove to a paper-towelled rack to drain. Serve with wedges of fresh lemon and tartar sauce.

CALAMARI PARMIGIANO

4 calamari steaks, pounded thin
Egg wash (one beaten egg)
1/4 cup flavored bread crumbs
4 tblsp. garlic flavored extra virgin olive oil
1 cup marinara sauce
2 tblsp. romano cheese
2 tblsp. parmesan cheese
4 tblsp. shredded mozzarella cheese

Preheat oven to 400 degrees. Pound and dredge calamari in egg wash and dip in bread crumbs. Saute in oil for 5 to 10 minutes, turning once. Place in baking dish. Pour marinara sauce over top. Top with romano, parmesan and mozzarella cheese. Bake until cheese melts, about 15 minutes. Serve immediately.

SEAFOOD BACCALA

A favorite holiday dish in Italy, baccala is traditionally made with salted dried cod. This is reconstituted by rinsing and soaking in fresh water that's changed every day for three days. But that original recipe was created back in the days before refrigeration and air delivery. The Seafood Baccala here — with ono or mahimahi — does not require any tedious rinsing and soaking procedures.

- 1/4 cup garlic flavored extra virgin olive oil
- 1/4 cup herb flour for dredging
- 2 lbs. fresh mahimahi or ono, cut in 2-inch diagonal strips
- 2 medium yellow onions, peeled and diced
- 1 slice bacon, diced
- 1 cup marinara sauce
- 1/2 cup Italian white wine
- 1 tsp. kosher salt
- Freshly ground black pepper
- 4 medium potatoes, diced (optional)

Preheat oven to 400 degrees. Dredge fish in herb flour. In a cast iron skillet, saute fish in oil 5 minutes. Turn fish; add onion, bacon, salt and pepper. Saute 5 minutes. Add wine and cook down completely. Add marinara sauce. Place pan in oven 5 minutes until mixture bubbles. Serve immediately.

NOTE: If desired, add potatoes by cooking in skillet before adding fish.

ZUPPA DI CLAMS (OR MUSSELS)

1 tblsp. cooked garlic
2 tblsp. garlic flavored extra virgin olive oil
Pinch crushed red pepper (optional)
24 clams (or mussels)
1 tsp. dried or fresh oregano
½ cup marinara sauce

Wash and clean clams well, using your nose to check for bad ones. Drain. In a heavy saucepan add garlic, oil (and pepper). Bring sauce to a simmer. Add marinara sauce. Allow to thicken over low heat, uncovered. Add oregano. Turn heat to high. Add clams. Cover with tight lid and allow clams to steam open for 5-10 minutes. Remove unopened clams from pot and discard. Turn off heat, replace lid and let stand warm, 5 minutes. Can be served in a bowl with crusty bread or placed over linguine.

To remove any trace of iodine taste, purge the shellfish in a salt water bath as in the Baked Clams Areginata recipe in Appetizers. Steaming the clams or mussels in the sauce accomplishes a couple of things besides just opening them up. It lets you find the bad ones — those that don't open — while the juices from the shellfish thin the sauce to a soupier consistency.

SHRIMP SAN MARZANO

While I recommend large tiger prawns here, there are alternatives. At Castagnola's, for example, we also use Kahuku shrimp, which are grown in man-made ponds on Oahu's north shore. The good news: Kahuku shrimp are definitely tastier. The bad news: they're also smaller and harder to remove from the shell. There's more waste and as a result, the local product is generally more expensive than the tiger prawns.

1 cup marinara sauce (1/2 cup if served without pasta)
2 lbs. shrimp, shelled and deveined
1/4 cup herb flour for dredging
1/4 cup garlic flavored extra virgin olive oil
1 tsp. hot pepper (optional)

Toss shrimp in herb flour. Saute shrimp in oil at high heat for 5 to 10 minutes. Remove shrimp. Add marinara sauce and hot pepper to pan. Simmer 5 minutes. Place shrimp on hot plate. Pour sauce on top and serve. Serve with pasta, if desired.

Floating a large fleet of charter skippers, the bountiful waters off the Big Island's Kona Coast yield some of the best-eating fish anywhere. In September 1989, I landed this 148-pound ahi (yellowfin tuna) from the sportfisher Black Bart.

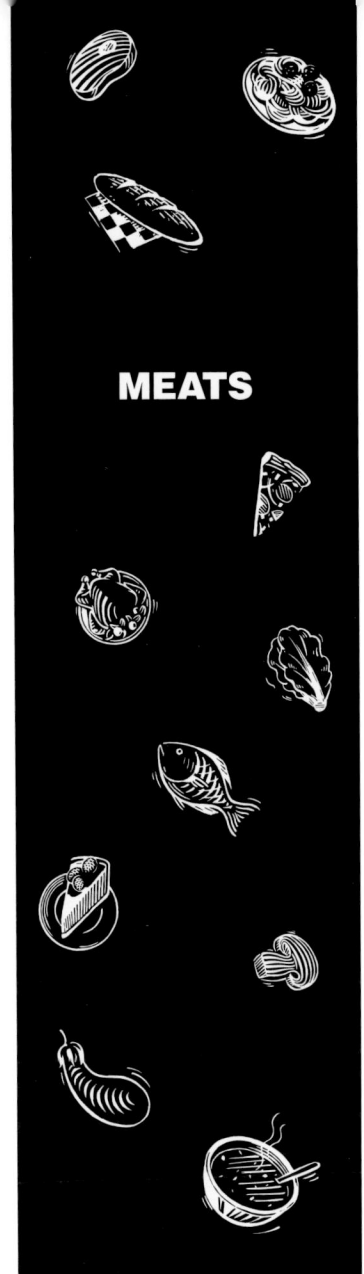

MEATS

Veal Sorrentino

Even in the middle of Hawaiian summer, Tuesday afternoon finds me shivering in 40-degree temperatures. That's because Tuesday's the day that Castagnola's chilled beef arrives in town.

In a meat locker not far from Honolulu Harbor, I personally inspect each side of the corn-fed western beef. If the fatty side of the meat is very hard to the touch, that means a high fat concentration throughout the entire piece. So for starters, the meat should be uniformly soft.

I also check for large lumps of fat. If I don't find any, it means a better distribution of marbled fat throughout the meat, which in turn insures an even distribution of flavor. Large pockets of fat mean that the rest of the meat is leaner. And the less fat, the less flavor.

Of course, chances are you don't have your own meat locker at home. But there are still many steps you can take to find fresh, top-quality meats for your own kitchen.

The key word here is "fresh." Remember that freezing will burst the tiny veins and capillaries in meat. When it thaws, the blood runs out and takes much of the flavor and nutrition with it.

At the butcher's, or the supermarket's specialty counter, don't just grab what's on the shelf. Ask for a different size and have it cut fresh for you. And don't buy meat which has already been ground. Buy a fresh round or chuck steak and have the butcher grind it for you. Only then can you be sure it's been ground fresh that day.

Buy a whole rack of lamb and cut the chops as you need them. For steaks, buy the meat in a roast, then cut it and trim it at home. The butcher can even crack the bone for you. Air starts deteriorating food immediately, so the longer you can delay that process, the better.

And what do we do at Castagnola's when our meat comes in frozen or uneven? Simple: we just take it off the menu for a day or two and feature the alternatives. I strongly suggest that you do the same!

VEAL SORRENTINO

Tender young Italian veal is one of the real joys of Italian cooking. Even the more mature variety available in the U.S. can make excellent veal dishes, depending upon freshness and grade. But let the buyer beware: I often question the quality of the veal I see selling at supermarket meat counters. At Castagnola's we buy it by the round and slice our veal steaks from that. And my bushy eyebrows always raise a bit when I find the supermarket's retail price to be less per pound than we pay for an entire round. Especially with veal, you definitely get what you pay for.

The recipes on the following pages represent some of the most popular veal dishes we serve at Castagnola's.

4 slices peeled eggplant, cut lengthwise, salted and rinsed
Egg wash
3/4 cup flavored bread crumbs
1/4 cup garlic flavored extra virgin olive oil
1 lb. mushrooms, sliced
4 scallopine of veal, 6 oz. each
6 tblsp. cold butter
4 tsp. parmesan cheese
4 tblsp. grated mozzarella cheese
1/2 cup dry marsala wine

Preheat oven to 400 degrees. Dredge eggplant in egg wash and bread crumbs. Saute in oil. Remove to heated serving platter. In same pan, saute sliced mushrooms over low heat until done. Put aside. Dredge scallopine in egg wash and flavored bread crumbs. Saute over low heat until done on both sides. Remove to serving platter. Place veal in roasting pan brushed with extra virgin olive oil. Top each scallopine with eggplant, a dab of butter, parmesan and mozzarella cheese and a drizzle of marsala wine. Bake until cheese melts. Return mushrooms to pan, add marsala wine and cook it down. Cut in butter, stir until mixture foams. Remove veal mixture from oven and put in serving dish. Pour mushroom and marsala sauce over top of veal.

VEAL PARMIGIANO

4 scallopine of veal, 6 oz. each
Egg wash
¾ cup flavored bread crumbs
¼ cup garlic flavored extra virgin olive oil
4 tblsp. mozzarella cheese
4 tsp. parmesan cheese
20 oz. marinara sauce if served without pasta (1 qt. with pasta)

Preheat oven to 450 degrees. Dip veal in egg wash and bread crumbs. In a cast iron skillet saute in oil over low heat 4 to 5 minutes per side. Place in baking dish brushed with olive oil and top with marinara sauce. (Just use skillet as baking pan if preparing for fewer than four people.) Top each scallopine with I tblsp. mozzarella cheese and 1 tsp. parmesan cheese. Bake until cheese melts and sauce bubbles. Serve with pasta.

I use cast iron skillets almost exclusively. Cast iron cooks the ingredients evenly and because the handle is also made of iron, you can simply use the same skillet in the oven as your baking pan. What's more, there's added nutritional value: the cast iron adds iron to whatever you're cooking.

VEAL MARSALA

Note that the cooking times given in these pages are approximate, since oven temperatures and even the internal temperatures of different cuts of meat can vary. Use your personal taste and common sense to judge when meat is cooked just right.

Egg wash (one beaten egg)
$1/2$ cup garlic flavored bread crumbs
4 tblsp. garlic flavored extra virgin olive oil
4 scallopine of veal, about 6 oz. each
1 lb. fresh mushrooms, sliced
$1/8$ cup dry marsala wine
4 tsp. butter

Dredge veal in egg wash and bread crumbs. In a cast iron skillet saute mushrooms in garlic flavored extra virgin olive oil. Remove from pan. Set aside. Saute veal, 1 or 2 at a time. Remove to heated serving dish. Add marsala wine, turning up flame. Add mushrooms back into wine. When wine starts bubbling, cut in butter. Stir rapidly until mixture foams. Pour over veal.

VEAL FRANCESE

1½ lbs. veal, sliced ¼-inch and pounded to ⅛-inch thick
1 cup flavored bread crumbs
2 eggs
¼ cup Italian white wine
Juice of one lemon
1 tsp. salt
1 tsp. freshly ground black pepper
Lemon wedges for garnish
Parsley for garnish
4 tblsp. garlic flavored extra virgin olive oil

Dredge veal in egg wash and deeply inbed in bread crumbs. In a cast iron skillet, saute veal scallopines in oil one at a time over very low heat. Remove to heated dish. Retain pan juices. Stir white wine, salt and pepper over heat. In same pan, add lemon juice. When it comes to a boil, pour gingerly over veal scallopines. Garnish with lemon wedges and parsley.

VEAL ANNA O'NEAL

This one is a spin-off of the classic Veal Sorrentino. One evening, Honolulu resident Anna O'Neal — a Castagnola's regular — asked for Sorrentino with a tomato sauce rather than the Marsala wine sauce. I liked the concept: a combination of eggplant and Veal Parmigiano. Anna liked the result, as did many others after it became a regular menu item. Today, we also serve Chicken Anna O'Neal and Beef Anna O'Neal.

4 slices peeled eggplant, cut lengthwise, salted and rinsed
Flavored bread crumbs
Egg wash (one beaten egg)
1/4 cup garlic flavored extra virgin olive oil
1 lb. mushrooms, sliced
4 scallopine of veal, 6 oz. each
1/2 cup mozzarella cheese
4 tsp. parmesan cheese
20 oz. marinara sauce if served without pasta (1 qt. with pasta)

Preheat oven to 400 degrees. Dredge eggplant in egg wash and bread crumbs. In a cast iron skillet, saute in oil. Set aside. Saute mushrooms over low heat; set aside. Dredge veal scallopine in egg wash and bread crumbs. Saute and set aside. Layer in a baking dish brushed with olive oil: veal, eggplant, marinara sauce, 1 tsp. parmesan per serving. (Just use skillet as baking pan if preparing for fewer than four people.) Bake until cheese melts over top and sauce bubbles. Serve with pasta.

VEAL PICCATA

Egg wash (one beaten egg)
½ cup herb flour
¼ cup garlic flavored extra virgin olive oil
4 scallopine of veal, 6 oz. each
2 tblsp. capers, rinsed in water
Juice of one lemon
¼ cup Italian white wine
4 tblsp. cold butter

Dredge veal in egg wash and herbed flour. In a cast iron skillet, saute veal in olive oil, one or two at a time. Remove to heated serving dish. Add capers and wine. Cook down. Add lemon juice. Cut butter into mixture until it foams. Pour over top of veal.

You may notice that the Veal Piccata sauce becomes darker in the cast iron skillet than in a white metal pan. It's no less tasty, however, and you're getting the added nutritional value of the iron, too.

VEAL AND PEPPERS

1½ lbs. veal, cut in 2-inch cubes about ½-inch thick
Herb flour for dredging
1 red bell pepper, seeded and cut in 1-inch strips
2 green bell peppers, seeded and cut in 1-inch strips
1 yellow onion, chopped coarsely
½ cup garlic flavored extra virgin olive oil
1 cup Bolla Valpolicella red wine
Salt and pepper to taste

Heat oil to frying temperature in a cast iron skillet. Saute onion and peppers and set aside. Saute veal in the flavored oil remaining in skillet. Add onion, peppers, salt and pepper. Simmer 10 to 15 minutes. Add veal and stir; add wine. Cook down, reduce by half. Cover pan and simmer on low heat 25 minutes.

The Veal and Peppers recipe is an excellent way to use the trimmings and small ends of the veal cut for scallopine. While we always use Bolla at Castagnola's, any good Italian Valpolicella will do.

VEAL CHOPS IN PEPPERS

4 veal chops, 1-inch thick
3 green bell peppers, seeded and julienned
3 red bell peppers, seeded and julienned
1/4 cup garlic flavored extra virgin olive oil
1 tsp. kosher salt
Fresh ground black pepper
1/4 cup herb flour

In cast iron skillet, saute peppers in oil with salt and pepper. When peppers are evenly browned, remove from pan. Dredge veal chops in herb flour and cook one or two at a time in the saucepan, 10 minutes per side. Return peppers to pan, cover with tight lid, and simmer for 20 minutes. Serve with potatoes or pasta.

OSSO BUCCO MILANESE

4-5 osso bucco veal shanks, cut 2½ inches thick, about 10-12 oz. each
¼ cup extra virgin olive oil
¼ cup herb flour for dredging
2 yellow onions, diced fine
1 tblsp. sugar
1 cup Italian white wine
½ cup chicken stock
¼ cup marinara sauce
1 tsp. kosher salt
Fresh ground black pepper
Lemon wheels
4 sprigs Italian parsley

Dust osso bucco in flour. Saute in oil in heavy saucepan, 5 to 10 minutes per side until browned. Set aside. Add onion to pan and simmer 15 minutes until lightly browned. Add sugar and simmer 5 minutes. Add wine and cook down 5 minutes. Add osso bucco, stock, marinara sauce, parsley, salt and pepper. Cover with a tight lid and simmer 1 hour until meat starts to peel from the bone. Serve on a bed of risotto Milanese. Top each osso bucco with sauce from pan. Garnish with lemon wheels and parsley.

In Hawaiian, a hole is a *puka*. The Italian word comes pretty close to that; it's *bucco* (boo-koh). Here's that old Italian favorite, Osso Bucco, "bone with a hole."

OXTAILS CACCIATORE

Oxtails don't really come from oxen at all. More accurately, they should be called steertails. It's one cut of beef that's OK to buy frozen, since there's very little blood content in this part of the animal.

As a specialty item, oxtail is universally popular, and Hawaii is no exception. Oxtail soup is a fixture on cafe and coffee shop menus throughout the islands. Oxtail makes an exceptional soup stock for beef bouillon, beef barley soup or any other beef-based soup. For this purpose, in fact, I can recommend it over just about any other cut of meat.

4 lbs. oxtails
$1/2$ cup herb flour
$1/4$ cup garlic flavored extra virgin olive oil
1 medium size yellow onion, chopped coarsely
1 tsp. sugar
2 cups water
1 sprig Italian parsley
1 red bell pepper, seeded and julienned
1 green bell pepper, seeded and julienned
5 - 10 Greek olives, pitted
$1/4$ cup Italian red wine
1 cup marinara sauce

Dust oxtails with herb flour. Brown in oil. Add onion until browned. Add sugar and simmer. Add water and parsley. Cover with a tight lid and simmer for 45 minutes. Add more water if necessary, enough to keep meat covered. Strain liquid into stainless steel bowl and cool to room temperature. Refrigerate at least 12 hours. Remove fat from stock. Trim all excess fat from oxtails. In heavy bottomed sauce pan, simmer stock, oxtails, peppers and olives in oil until peppers are browned. Add $1/4$ cup wine. Simmer 10 minutes. Add marinara sauce and 1 cup stock and cover with a tight lid. Cook 1 hour or until meat starts to fall off bone.

BONELESS PORK CACCIATORE

- 1½ – 2 lbs. sliced pork butt, sliced ¼-inch thick and trimmed of all fat
- ¼ – ½ cup herb flour
- ½ cup garlic flavored extra virgin olive oil
- 1 red bell pepper, julienned and seeded
- 1 green bell pepper, julienned and seeded
- 1 medium yellow onion, chopped coarsely
- 5 - 10 Greek olives, pitted
- 1 cup marinara sauce
- ¼ cup Italian red wine
- Kosher salt
- Freshly ground black pepper
- Fresh or dried basil

Trim pork slices of fat and cut into 2-inch-square pieces. Dust in herb flour. In a cast iron skillet saute in oil for just 5 minutes on each side. Set aside. Add peppers, onion and Greek olives to pan. Saute until peppers are done, about 10 to 15 minutes. Add red wine, olives and cooked pork slices. Simmer 5 minutes. Add marinara sauce. Cover with tight lid and reduce heat to simmer. Cook for ½ hour to 1 hour.

PORK OR BEEF BRACIOLE

About the only time I was early at the dinner table was when my mother was serving this dish. It's my all-time favorite.

Made with either beef or pork, this rolled delicacy is a favored dish in southern Italian kitchens. In Pork Braciole, I recommend using pork butt for the extra moisture the fat provides. The meat can be pounded flat with any hammer. At Castagnola's, I use a stainless steel repair mallet from an auto body shop!

8 slices pork butt (or chuck or round of beef) cut 1/4-inch thick, about 4 inch x 8 inch
4 oz. pinole (pine) nuts
4 oz. grated parmesan cheese
2 oz. unseeded white raisins
1 bunch Italian parsley
Kosher salt
Freshly ground black pepper
1/2 cup herb flour
1/4 cup garlic flavored extra virgin olive oil
8 oz. Italian red wine
2 red bell peppers
1 green bell pepper
1/2 lb. sliced mushrooms
8 pitted Greek olives
2 cups marinara sauce
   (4 cups if served with pasta)

Lay pork or beef on board. Sprinkle lightly with salt and pepper. Place 5 to 6 raisins evenly on top of each piece. With heavy hammer or mallet, pound down to 1/8-inch thickness. Sprinkle each piece with parmesan, nuts and parsley. Roll each piece tightly lengthwise from widest to narrowest end of meat. Tie with heavy butcher cord. Dust in flour. Saute in oil until slightly browned. Return to sauce pan. Cover with marinara sauce, or for cacciatore style, add peppers, mushrooms, olives and red wine. Cover with tight lid. Simmer for 1 hour. Remove butcher cord on the serving plate. Serve with pasta.

TRIPE NAPOLENTANO

- 2½ lbs. honeycomb tripe
- 2 yellow onions, peeled and diced
- ¼ cup garlic flavored extra virgin olive oil
- 2 cups cold water
- ¼ cup white vinegar
- 2 tsp. kosher salt
- Freshly ground black pepper
- 1 cup marinara sauce
- ¼ cup Italian white wine
- 1 tsp. crushed red pepper (optional)

In water, boil whole tripe and 1 tsp. salt for 15 minutes. Remove and allow to cool. Rinse 2 to 3 times with water. Cut tripe into strips ½-inch thick and 2 inches long. In a stainless steel or ceramic bowl, add water and vinegar. Mix well. Add tripe slices and let stand for 45 minutes. Rinse tripe well and pat dry. In heavy saucepan simmer tripe and onions in oil, stirring constantly over low heat for 25 minutes. Add wine and reduce for 10 minutes. Add marinara sauce, 1 tsp. salt and pepper (and red pepper). Simmer 2 hours on low heat. Taste tripe for preferred tenderness. Serve as appetizer or with pasta.

Prepared properly, tripe is a real delicacy, but only if it's fresh. With tripe, the difference between fresh and frozen is even more pronounced than with other parts of the animal.

The vinegar bath outlined here is an important step. The same process used by French chefs in cleaning escargot, it's an excellent way to wash away any traces of acid from the animal's stomach lining.

MEATBALLS

Rather than rely on pre-ground meats, buy a roast and ask the butcher to grind it for you while you wait. Better yet, grind it yourself. I highly recommend the Kitchen Aid, one of the best culinary investments you can make. Buy a six-pound roast, grind three pounds for meatballs, and the other three pounds will keep well in your refrigerator.

Be sure to cook the onions before you mix them with the ground meat. Raw onions, especially those in the center, will stay that way, even when the meatball is cooked.

The chicken meatballs were added to our menu in late 1988, during the brouhaha over beef fed with hormones. When our chicken supplier guaranteed there were none in his product, we introduced them as a hormone-free alternative.

2 lbs. ground meat, fresh ground round preferred
1 cup flavored bread crumbs
2 eggs
2 yellow onions, quartered, cooked and chopped fine
5 sprigs chopped Italian parsley
2 tsp. romano cheese

Preheat oven to 300 degrees. Mix all ingredients well and put in refrigerator to cool.

Shape meatballs into 3-inch, 3-ounce balls. Place in roasting pan brushed with garlic flavored olive oil. Bake 25 minutes. Cool.

Can be made with sausage, ground beef or ground chicken. Meatballs can be added to marinara sauce, then cooked another 15 to 20 minutes before serving.

NOTE: Chilling the meat makes it much easier to handle and the meatballs will hold their shape better when cooking, too.

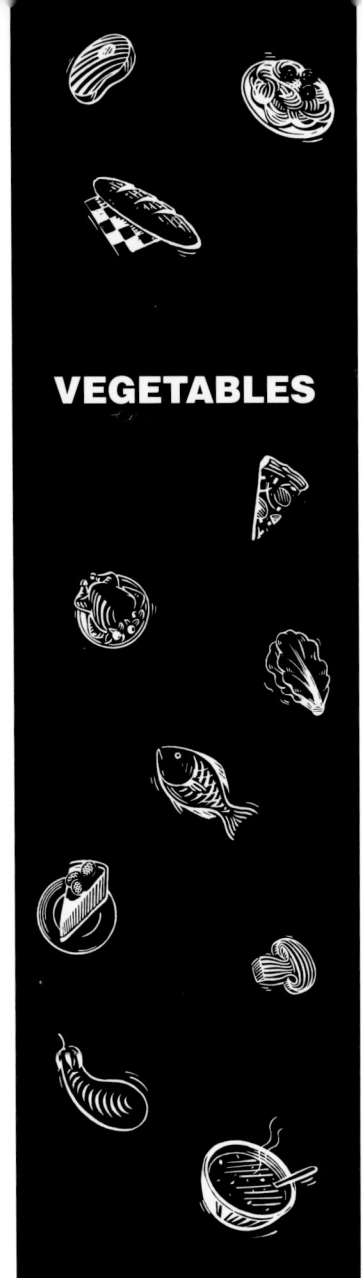

VEGETABLES

Baked Stuffed Eggplant Parmigiano

Preceding page, clockwise from top:
Espresso, Cannoli, Almond Cookies, Ricotta Cheesecake, Tiramisu and Zabaglione

The Italian cook has a way with vegetables. Working with simple, time-honored cooking methods, he or she can turn the common eggplant or tomato into a culinary work of art.

The raw materials should be as fresh as possible, of course, even if you have to buy them off the back of a farmer's pickup truck at the local People's Open Market. The chances are better that these vegetables have ripened the Italian way — on the vine and not in storage.

In Italy, a vegetable is something more than just a side dish. Often it is served on its own plate *a contorno* — to "round out" the meal. Here are flavors so rich and delicate they can steal the show from the main course.

On the following pages, we present two great ways to prepare eggplant, Potatoes Castagnola, Escarole Saute, Sauteed Zucchini and a rich marinade for raw vegetables.

POTATOES CASTAGNOLA

I love potatoes. My mother, who was French, always made them with a little thyme. Today, I still savor a hint of that aromatic seasoning in potatoes. Of course, she also prepared them more like French fries while at Castagnola's, our potatoes are mostly cut stew-style.

If you have a Dutch oven, this dish can put it to good use. Otherwise, a cast iron skillet or any heavy saucepan will do.

- 4 large red potatoes, peeled and cut into eighths
- 2 medium sized yellow onions, peeled and sliced 1-inch thick
- 3 tblsp. extra virgin olive oil
- 1 tsp. kosher salt
- 1 tsp. dried basil
- 1/8 tsp. powdered thyme
- 1 tsp. black pepper

Saute onions in pan with oil. Remove and set aside. Saute potatoes, salt, pepper, basil and thyme. Simmer with tight lid 25 minutes, browning evenly. Add onions to pan. Simmer 25 minutes more, taste for doneness of potato and serve.

EGGPLANT MILANESE

1 large eggplant, peeled and sliced 1/4-inch thick
1 tblsp. kosher salt
Egg wash (one beaten egg)
1/4 cup flavored Italian bread crumbs
1/4 cup garlic flavored extra virgin olive oil
1/8 cup Italian white wine
1 tsp. kosher salt
Freshly ground black pepper

Sprinkle salt on each slice of eggplant. Place on plate and cover with another plate for 25 minutes. Squeeze and drain eggplant; pat dry. Dip in egg wash and dredge in bread crumbs. In a cast iron skillet saute over low heat on both sides in oil. Add wine, salt and pepper. Simmer 5 minutes. Place on serving platter and serve with pan juices.

SAUTEED ZUCCHINI

2 lbs. zucchini, sliced at a 45 degree angle, 1/4-inch thick
1/4 cup extra virgin olive oil
1 tsp. kosher salt
Freshly ground black pepper
Fresh parsley

Wash and slice zucchini diagonally, 1/4-inch thick. In a cast iron skillet saute in oil with salt and pepper. Saute 5 minutes on each side and serve immediately. Pour oil over top. Garnish with parsley.

BAKED STUFFED EGGPLANT PARMIGIANO

At Castagnola's we use almost a case of eggplant every day. That's partly because there are so many vegetarians in health-conscious Hawaii. This versatile vegetable can stand alone — like the recipes here — or enhance many other dishes.

Salting and squeezing eggplant helps remove that slightly bitter taste. Always begin with this important step.

Many chefs carve their Baked Stuffed Eggplant Parmigiano out like a potato. I prefer mine sliced and prepared sandwich-style, which makes for easier handling.

1 large eggplant, peeled and sliced 1/4-inch thick lengthwise
Egg wash (one beaten egg)
1/2 cup flavored bread crumbs
2 slices eggplant, diced
1/8 cup garlic flavored extra virgin olive oil
4 tblsp. ricotta cheese
8 tsp. parmesan cheese
4 tblsp. mozzarella cheese
1 cup marinara sauce

Sprinkle salt on each slice of eggplant. Place on plate and cover with another plate for 25 minutes. Squeeze and drain eggplant; pat dry. Dip slices in egg wash and bread crumbs. Saute in oil. Set aside. Saute diced eggplant in oil until well done, about 15 minutes. Set aside to cool. On each eggplant slice, place 1 tblsp. ricotta, diced eggplant and 1 tsp. of parmesan. Top with another slice of eggplant matched in size and place in saucepan. Repeat process with remaining slices. Cover with marinara sauce, and to each portion add 1 tsp. mozzarella and remainder of 1 tsp. parmesan cheese. Place in 350-degree oven until cheese melts and sauce starts to bubble.

NOTE: Save the larger slices of eggplant for serving and the smaller end slices for the filling.

ESCAROLE SAUTE

1-2 heads escarole, broken into large pieces, washed and patted dry
¼ cup garlic flavored extra virgin olive oil
1 tsp. kosher salt
Freshly ground black pepper
1 tsp. crushed dry red pepper (optional)

In heavy bottomed pan, saute escarole in oil with salt and pepper (and crushed red pepper). Stir frequently. As escarole starts to wilt down, cover with tight lid. Reduce heat and saute another 15 minutes until done.

The broad-leafed variety of endive, escarole is a big favorite in Italy. In Hawaii, however, it's a scarce commodity and we often substitute romaine lettuce at Castagnola's.

The Escarole Saute recipe can also be used to make Escarole and Bean Soup (see Pasta Fagiole). Simply add beans to the sauteed escarole and let it simmer for 20 minutes.

MARINADE FOR RAW VEGETABLES

1 qt. distilled water
1 qt. white vinegar
2 tsp. kosher salt
2 tsp. sugar
1 oz. garlic cloves
1 tsp. crushed dried red peppers or 2 chopped chili peppers

Blend all ingredients in blender and strain. Pour over raw sliced mixed vegetables, carrots, peppers, celery, etc. Store in non-metal container.

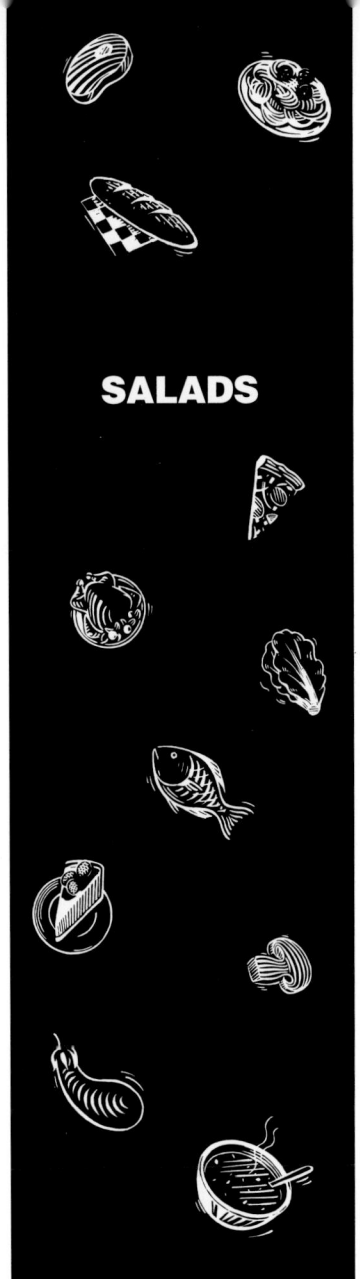

In Italy, salads epitomize the pure, classic qualities of Italian cooking. Here you'll find simple seasonings, compatible ingredients and straightforward presentations. The flavors are clean and sparkling, without sticky, cloying salad dressings. And in Italian salads, the beauty of using only extra virgin olive oil is most apparent.

In formal Italian dinners, the salad is usually served as an accompaniment to the meat course. Often, it's no more than a simple escarole with a little extra virgin olive oil and red wine vinegar. Closer to home, of course, it stands alone earlier in the meal and can even serve as the main course.

Here you'll find pasta and calamari salads, as well as the classic tossed and Caesar salads.

COLD PASTA SALAD

When preparing Cold Pasta Salad, be sure to cut meats and julienne vegetables in the same shape as the pasta you're using. This step adds immeasurably to the overall presentation.

1 lb. linguine
2 qts. water
1 tsp. kosher salt
1 tblsp. extra virgin olive oil
Romaine lettuce
4 slices prosciutto, julienned
1 roasted red bell pepper cut in 1/2-inch wide strips
8 pitted Greek black olives
1 large or 2 medium fresh tomatoes, cut in wedges
4 oz. fontinella cheese cut in 1/2-inch by 2-inch triangles
2 tblsp. Italian dressing per serving

Cook pasta in water with salt. Drain and toss with oil. Set aside and allow to cool. Place pasta in bowls on bed of lettuce. To each serving add 2 slices prosciutto, 3 slices pepper, olives, tomato wedges and 2 slices cheese. Top with Italian dressing and serve.

COLD CALAMARI SALAD

1 qt. water
2 giant calamari steaks, 6 oz. each
1 oz. fresh garlic
1 tsp. oregano
1 tsp. kosher salt
Freshly ground black pepper
Juice of 1/2 lemon
1/4 cup oregano flavored olive oil

Add 1/2 oz. garlic, 1/2 tsp. oregano, salt and pepper to water. Simmer 1 hour over low heat. Add calamari and poach for 5 minutes over low temperature. Cool 5 minutes with burner off. Remove calamari and cool at room temperature. Slice calamari at a diagonal across the steak as thinly as possible. Toss in marinade.

For marinade, crush remaining garlic in wooden or stainless steel bowl. Add remaining oregano, pepper, salt, lemon juice and oil. Marinate calamari slices 1/2 hour at room temperature. Refrigerate. Serve cold with lemon wheels on bed of lettuce. Garnish with fresh parsley.

CAESAR SALAD

If you don't think of Caesar Salad as Italian, you're not alone. Fact is, it was created in Mexico by an Italian chef, who adapted his grandmother's original recipe. In all my travels throughout Italy, however, I have yet to see anything like it on a menu.

None of which has prevented Caesar Salad from being a big favorite at Castagnola's. The secret is in the anchovies: use them sparingly and you can barely taste them. Even people who hate anchovies — like my wife, Ruth — think they're wonderful in Caesar Salad.

Try to find a market that keeps their canned anchovies refrigerated. Anchovies kept on unrefrigerated shelves tend to go rancid even if in sealed cans.

- 1 oz. or 6 cloves fresh peeled garlic
- 2 to 3 anchovy fillets depending on size, 2-inches long
- 4 tsp. imported romano cheese
- 2 egg yolks
- Dash tabasco sauce
- Dash worcestershire sauce
- Juice of one lemon
- 1/4 cup extra virgin olive oil
- 4 heaping tsp. croutons
- Full head romaine lettuce

Wash and dry lettuce and break into pieces. Use a wooden bowl and stiff fork to crush the garlic. Garlic can then be left in bowl or removed depending upon your tolerance to garlic. Add anchovies and crush into a powdery paste. Add romano cheese and crush into an even smooth texture. Add two egg yolks, tabasco, worcestershire, lemon juice and olive oil. Add pieces of lettuce, top with croutons and toss well.

NOTE: Because of the threat of salmonella, I recommend brown eggs, since there's less chance that salmonella bacteria will penetrate their thicker shells. Also, try washing eggs with a little white vinegar.

TOSSED SALAD

- 1 head romaine or escarole lettuce, broken into bite-sized pieces
- 4 oz. coarsely diced fontinella cheese
- 4 wedges fresh garden-ripe tomato per serving
- 1 tblsp. marinated vegetables per serving
- 2 tblsp. Italian dressing per serving

Mix all ingredients and top with fresh ground pepper and dressing.

If escarole lettuce were as readily available in Hawaii as it is on the East Coast, we'd use it in most of our salads, as the Italians do. But even at Castagnola's, I'm lucky if I can get escarole three or four times a year — this from a small farmer in Manoa Valley.

Romaine lettuce is a legitimate substitute, however, and there's no problem getting it, either. We could always ship in escarole from the East Coast, but the produce would be wilted. And in Italian cooking, of course, freshness is more important than the type of produce you use.

VINAIGRETTE SALAD DRESSING

- 1 pt. extra virgin olive oil
- 1 pt. red wine vinegar
- 4 tsp. kosher salt
- 4 tsp. fresh ground pepper
- 4 tsp. sugar
- 1 oz. fresh peeled garlic
- 1 tsp. dried basil leaves

Add to blender in sequence and blend until smooth. Strain out any lumps in garlic. Refrigerate.

SOUPS

A rich, hearty Italian soup can set the tone for the entire meal. For best results, don't forget to flavor the water overnight before cooking — with beans, meat, vegetables or whatever the recipe calls for. In this way, your flavorful, seasoned stock is ready to go when you are. Pre-flavoring of stock is universal, whether they're making beef bouillon in France, pot liquors down South or gefilte fish in New York.

The soups in this chapter range from a rich Vichyssoise to creamy vegetable soups to very hearty bean, beef and pepper dishes.

PASTA FAGIOLE

Pasta Fagiole is pronounced "fa-jole" most places in Italy except around Naples, where it's "va-zool." Remember Dean Martin singing that Neapolitan favorite, *That's Amore?* "When the stars make you drool just like Pasta Va-zool, that's amore..."

This bean soup is a nutritional dish at a very economical price. In blue-collar Italian communities, in fact, it can be a real staple of life.

You can use any bean you'd like, but pinto beans rank highest nutritionally and as a result, that's what we use at Castagnola's.

1 lb. pinto beans
1 1/4 qts. water
2 smoked ham hocks
1 tsp. kosher salt
1 tsp. freshly ground black pepper
1 large yellow onion, peeled and diced
6 cloves garlic, peeled
1/4 tsp. crushed red pepper (optional)
1 cup marinara sauce
1/4 cup garlic flavored extra virgin olive oil
4 oz. elbow or soup macaroni
1 tblsp. dried basil
Grated romano cheese

NOTE: To cut preparation time and eliminate overnight soaking, bring beans to a boil for 2 minutes, turn off heat and allow to cool covered tightly for one hour. If you'd like thicker soup, blend some of the beans with some soup from the pot, then add mixture back to pot.

Soak beans overnight in a large covered pot filled to the top with water. In heavy bottomed sauce pan, simmer ham hocks, garlic, onion, salt, pepper and dried basil, in one quart plus one cup of water. Cover; simmer on low heat for one hour. Allow to cool. Refrigerate overnight. The next day, remove ham hocks from pot, remove meat, dice and put bones aside. Add meat and beans which have been washed and drained back to pot. Cover and simmer on low heat for 1 1/2 hours. In cast iron skillet, saute bones and hot pepper in garlic flavored olive oil for 15 minutes. Add marinara sauce and simmer for 1/2 hour. Set aside until beans have cooked for 1 1/2 hours. Strain out bones, add marinara sauce to bean pot. Simmer for 1 hour or until beans are tender. To 2 quarts of boiling water add pasta and 1 tsp. salt. Cook, stirring frequently, 10 to 15 minutes, until pasta is al dente. Drain pasta and add to soup at serving time. Top with romano cheese.

VICHYSSOISE

- **1 large or 2 medium potatoes, peeled and diced**
- **1 bunch leeks, washed, trimmed and diced, saving dark green leaves for garnish**
- **1 tsp. kosher salt**
- **1/2 tsp. white pepper**
- **1 tblsp. chicken fat**
- **1 qt. chicken stock**
- **1 egg yolk**
- **1/2 cup half and half cream**

In a heavy bottomed sauce pan, saute potatoes and leeks until golden but not brown. Add salt and white pepper. Simmer 5 minutes. Add chicken stock. Bring to a boil, reduce heat and simmer until potatoes are soft. Strain off and retain 1 cup of chicken stock. Whisk to cool down. Whisk in egg yolk and cream. In a blender, mix potatoes and leeks together. Strain into a large bowl. Put back in pot, bring to simmer. Fold in cream mixture and whisk until cool. Serve in chilled bowls or glasses. Garnish with dark green finely chopped leek.

BEEF BARLEY SOUP

This one can be almost a meal in itself. I prefer using oxtails to make the stock, but you might also consider neck bones or beef marrow bones. Once again, it's best to prepare the stock the night before you cook the soup.

- 2 qts. water
- 2 lbs. oxtails
- 2 yellow onions, peeled and diced
- 1/4 cup herb flour
- 1/4 cup extra virgin olive oil
- 2 tsp. kosher salt
- Freshly ground black pepper
- 1 sprig parsley
- 1/2 cup barley, washed and strained

Wash oxtails. Drain, pat dry and dust oxtails in herb flour. In a heavy bottomed sauce pan, saute oxtails, onions, 1 tsp. salt and pepper in oil until oxtails are browned on all sides. Add water, 1 tsp. salt and parsley and simmer 2 hours. Remove from heat and let cool by itself. When cooled, strain and retain stock in stainless steel bowl. Place uncovered in refrigerator so fat forms on top of stock like ice. Remove excess fat from oxtails. Dice meat and retain. Remove fat from stock and place stock in pot. Add barley and let simmer 25 minutes, until barley is done to taste. Add diced oxtail meat and simmer 10 minutes.

CREAM OF MUSHROOM SOUP

- 1½ lbs. fresh mushrooms, sliced
- 2 tblsp. chicken fat or extra virgin olive oil
- 1 qt. chicken stock
- ½ cup half and half cream
- 1 egg yolk
- 1 tsp. kosher salt
- ½ tsp. white pepper

Saute mushrooms, salt and white pepper in heavy bottomed sauce pan for 20 minutes. Add stock and simmer 20 minutes. Strain off 1 cup of stock into stainless steel bowl. Allow to cool to room temperature. Whisk in egg yolk and cream. Set aside. In a blender, mix all but half of mushrooms with the stock. Return to saucepan with mushrooms and stock/cream/egg yolk mixture. Bring to a simmer and serve.

CREAM OF WATERCRESS SOUP

In Hawaii, we're fortunate in that watercress is a relatively plentiful commodity. But if there's none available, you can use this recipe for just about any cream of vegetable soup, such as broccoli, cauliflower or spinach.

- 2 lbs. fresh watercress, washed and drained, stems removed
- 2 medium red potatoes, peeled and diced
- 2 tblsp. chicken fat or extra virgin olive oil
- 1 qt. chicken stock
- 1 tsp. kosher salt
- 1/2 tsp. ground white pepper
- 1/2 cup half and half cream
- 1 egg yolk

In heavy bottomed sauce pan, saute potatoes until tender. In a separate pan, saute watercress. Add stock to potato pot and simmer, covered, for 25 minutes until potatoes are soft. Add watercress, salt and white pepper and let simmer another 10 minutes. Strain stock, retaining 1 cup. Put in a bowl and allow to cool to room temperature. Whisk in egg yolk and cream. In a blender, mix potatoes and half of the watercress. Run through strainer. Add cream mixture and remaining watercress, stir. Bring to just under a boil and serve immediately. Garnish with croutons.

PEPPER POT SOUP

- 1 lb. honeycomb tripe
- 2 cups water
- 1 tsp. salt
- 1/4 cup white vinegar
- 1/4 cup extra virgin olive oil
- 1 yellow onion, diced
- 1/4 cup Italian white wine
- 1/4 cup marinara sauce
- 1 cup chicken stock
- 2 large potatoes
- 2 red bell peppers, seeded and diced
- 1 sprig Italian parsley
- 1 tsp. kosher salt
- 1 tsp. crushed hot pepper (optional)

Wash tripe and boil in water with salt for 25 minutes. Drain and wash well, removing all fatty deposits. Dice into half-inch cubes. Soak in stainless steel or ceramic bowl with 2 cups water and 1/4 cup vinegar for 45 minutes. Drain and rinse well, at least 2 times. Place tripe in heavy bottomed sauce pan with oil and onions. Saute until onions are barely golden brown. Add tripe, saute 5 minutes, stirring well with onion. Add wine, cook down. Add stock and marinara sauce and simmer in heavy pot covered tightly for 2 hours. Add potatoes, pepper, parsley and salt and optional hot pepper. Simmer 25 minutes until potatoes are done. Serve with crusty garlic bread.

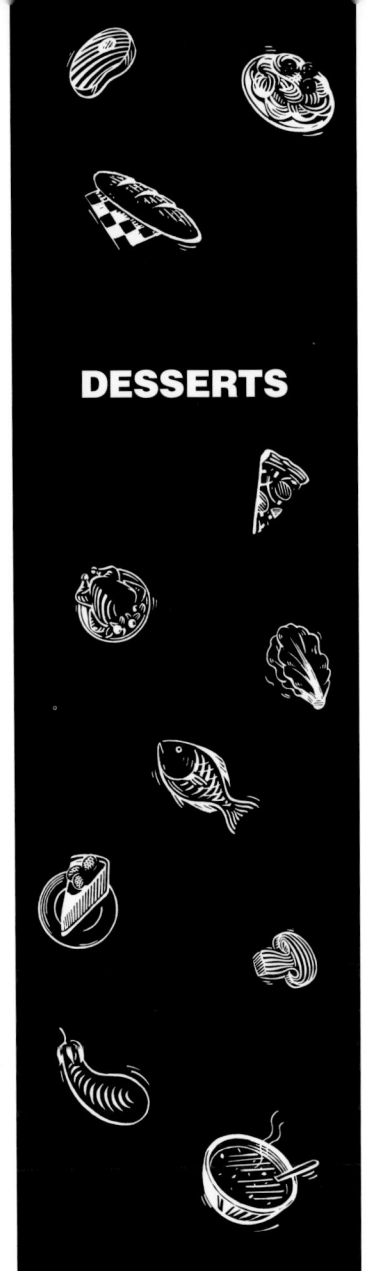

DESSERTS

Here is the crowning touch, the *finale alla Italia* which can be elegantly elaborate or as simple as fruit, cheese and nuts. Served with a good vintage port, in fact, the latter combination may be the most popular Italian dessert of all.

Dessert, Italian-style, can be complex and expensive. So in this final chapter, I've focused on those which can be easily prepared in the home. To make things even easier, consider a good all-purpose machine such as the Kitchen Aid by Hobart (see Meats), which can, for example, whip egg whites to a froth you'd never get by hand-beating.

Turn the page to some truly tempting desserts, from easy Almond Walnut Cookies to Zabaglione and Zapoli. In between are a variety of great ways to cap a memorable Italian dinner.

PORT WINE SERVED WITH CHEESE, FRUIT AND NUTS

This one is an Italian tradition. Select a good Portuguese port wine, and serve a sharp cheese like provolone or U.S.-made fontinella, similar to provolone but not quite as smoky. Or you can substitute a sharp cheddar or even bleu cheese, though of course, the latter isn't ideal for eating with the hands. Whatever you select, let it sit at room temperature for an hour before serving, to bring out the sharpness, full flavor and aroma.

On a plate arrange sliced peeled fruit, nuts (optional) and a very sharp cheese (fontinella or provolone is recommended). Serve with a glass of vintage Portuguese port wine.

ZAPOLI

1 3/4 cup flour
2 tblsp. sugar
1/2 tsp. salt
1/2 cup warm beer
2 oz. cake yeast or
 1 pkg. dry yeast

Hawaii residents are all familiar with malasadas, that sweet, deep-fried delicacy from Portugal. Zapoli is the Italian version, smaller and shaped like a teardrop. Enjoy!

Add yeast, sugar and salt to warm beer and stir until dissolved. Mix in flour, bread-making style, until a tight ball forms, and knead for ten minutes. Coat with a thin film of olive oil. Cover with plastic wrap. Let stand for one hour. Punch down and form into small teardrop shapes about the size of a half-dollar. Drop in hot oil two to four at a time. Fry until golden brown. Remove and drain. Dust with powdered sugar flavored with vanilla bean. Serve warm.

CANNOLI

1 1/3 cup flour
2 tsp. butter
Pinch of salt
1/2 tsp. sugar
1 egg yolk
1-2 tblsp. dry marsala wine
4 cannoli tubes
Egg wash (one beaten egg)
Peanut or olive oil

Filling:
1 lb. riccota cheese
1 cup sugar
1 tblsp. Cointreau liqueur or orange flavoring
1/2 cup chopped walnuts
4 tblsp. chopped chocolate

Mix all filling ingredients and refrigerate. Knead dough together, starting with dry ingredients. Form dough into ball, cover with warm towel and let sit for 1 hour. Roll out dough and cut into 4-inch squares less than 1/8-inch thick. Take a cannoli tube and roll it diagonally from corner to corner. Seal edges with egg wash. Deep fry one or two tubes at a time in oil until golden brown. Remove tubes from oil. Allow to cool on paper towel. Carefully remove tubes and stuff with filling just prior to serving. Top with confectioner's sugar flavored with vanilla bean.

This cream-filled pastry is a Sicilian classic, named for the cannon-shaped tubes used to form the dough. You can find cannoli tubes in a specialty shop or just buy one-inch-diameter aluminum tubing at a hardware store and cut it into approximately five-inch lengths.

When one of the characters in the first *Godfather* film leaves the house to put a hit on someone, his wife tells him not to forget the cannolis. It's the director's way of reminding us that these are regular guys just doing their jobs.

FRESH FRUIT WITH RUM SAUCE

Use a Jamaican rum, preferably Myers, for this piquant dessert. That particular rum provides the strongest flavor with the least alcohol content. If you'd like to skip the alcohol, rum flavoring will suffice, though of course all the alcohol will cook out anyway, leaving only the essence.

1 cup water
1 cup brown sugar
2 oz. heavy Jamaican Myers rum
Fruit of your choice
Whipped cream (optional)

Stir water and sugar over heat until liquid comes to a boil and clarifies. Allow to cool. Stir in rum. Place fruit in chilled dessert dishes. Top with rum sauce. Allow to sit 5 to 10 minutes and serve (topped with whipped cream).

ZABAGLIONE

This rich, frothy egg pudding gets its distinctive flavor from the marsala wine. You can serve it either hot or cold. What's more, you can add fruit on the bottom: cherries, strawberries, even pineapple. Use your imagination!

4 egg yolks
4 tsp. brown sugar
4 tblsp. dry marsala wine
Whipped cream

Whisk egg yolks in stainless steel bowl until bright yellow. Whip in sugar and wine. With pliers, hold bowl over pot of hot water (a double boiler can be used). Whisk vigorously until stiff peaks appear. Place in serving dishes. Top with whipped cream and sprinkle with brown sugar. Serve immediately, plain or on a bed of fresh fruit.
NOTE: This can be refrigerated and served cold.

ALMOND WALNUT COOKIES

1 cup flour
1 cup confectioners sugar
8 oz. chopped walnuts
Pinch of salt
1 egg, separated
3 oz. butter
1 tsp. almond extract
1-2 tblsp. milk

Preheat oven to 325 degrees. Mix flour, butter, sugar, walnuts and salt. Add egg yolk and mix well. Add almond extract and egg white. Add milk as needed until consistency is soft yet stiff. Insert mixture in pastry tube and squeeze out in drop-cookie fashion on baking sheet lined with Pam spray or parchment paper. Bake 14 minutes. Rotate tray after 8 minutes for even browning. Cool on cooling rack.

ITALIAN RICOTTA CHEESECAKE

Be sure to bake the bottom of the cheesecake until it's evenly browned — before you form and bake the rest of the cheesecake. Otherwise, the moist filling will make the bottom crust soggier than you'd like.

Ricotta cheese produces a lighter, more granular cheesecake. If you prefer it thicker and smoother, substitute marscapone or a good American cream cheese. But don't forget: using ricotta helps keep the calories down.

For Tart Dough:
1½ cups flour
3 oz. butter
9 tblsp. sugar
1 egg yolk
1 lemon, grated for the rind
Milk or water as needed

Filling:
3 lbs. ricotta cheese
2 egg yolks
5 whole eggs
1½ cups sugar
1 tsp. vanilla extract
6 oz. heavy cream

For filling: cut sugar in mixer with ricotta. Blend well. Add vanilla and whole eggs, one at a time, while increasing mixer speed. Add egg yolks and further increase mixing speed. Blend for 10 minutes. Remove from mixer, fold in cream and set aside.

Preheat oven to 350 degrees. Cut butter, sugar and flour together. Add egg yolk. Add lemon zest and milk or water to form thick dough. Cover and refrigerate dough. Spray and dust with flour a 12-inch springform pan. Cut dough ball in half. Roll out to fit pan. Bake 15 minutes until evenly browned, rotating pan bottom after 10 minutes. Remove to rack and allow to cool. Attach baked dough inside of springform pan. Cut and roll out remaining dough and evenly press around sides of pan, starting thick on bottom and tapering up to thin edge at top. Fill pan with filling mix. Bake 10 minutes at 350 degrees. Reduce oven temperature to 200 degrees and turn pan. Bake 1 hour. Shut oven off. Leave cheesecake in oven for 1 hour with door slightly open. Remove from oven and allow to cool in springform pan. Carefully remove from pan. Trim top of excess dough. Refrigerate at least 3 hours before cutting and serving.

CASTAGNACCIO

2 cups chopped walnuts
4 oz. chestnut paste
3 cups cake flour
1½ cups brown sugar
4 oz. butter
3 eggs
1 tblsp. rum flavoring
1 tblsp. baking powder
Pinch of kosher salt
⅛ tsp. baking soda
1 heaping tsp. ground cinnamon
1 cup buttermilk
Whipped cream (optional)

Preheat oven to 325 degrees. In a mixing bowl with a cake mixer, cut in butter with brown sugar until well blended. Add eggs and increase speed. Add rum flavoring; mix until creamy. Add chestnut paste. Reduce speed. Add dry ingredients alternately with enough buttermilk to reach consistency of heavy cake dough. Coat a 9 x 11 inch baking pan with olive oil or butter; dust with flour. Place cake mixture in pan. Bake for 30 to 45 minutes. When done, middle of cake should spring back. Cool on cake rack. Serve warm or reheated topped with rum sauce (and whipped cream).

NOTE: Buttermilk may be replaced by 1 cup of regular milk with 1 tblsp. white vinegar stirred in. Let stand for 25 minutes.

Castagnaccio is a chestnut cake. Taking liberties with my namesake dessert — Castagnola means chestnut — I've added chopped walnuts to this old favorite.

If you can't find chestnut paste, you can slit the shells of a pound of whole chestnuts, then boil them for 30 minutes. Remove the shells and run the chestnuts through your food processor with ½ cup of sugar.

TIRAMISU

Here's the most popular dessert served at Castagnola's, a richly layered cake flavored with rum and Kahlua. The cheese is marscapone, that delicate Italian cream cheese which, by the way, is delicious spread on a bagel. Tiramisu means "pick me up." This recipe serves 12.

3/4 cup sifted flour
3/4 cup granulated sugar
5 eggs, separated
1/2 tsp. baking powder
1/4 cup Dutch cocoa
Pinch of salt
1 tblsp. rum extract
1 tblsp. brewed espresso coffee
1 tblsp. beer (or water)

Filling:
18 oz. marscapone cheese
1 1/2 cups confectioner's sugar
3 cups heavy whipped cream
1 tblsp. rum extract
1 tblsp. confectioner's sugar
1 tblsp. cocoa

Topping:
2 tblsp. Myers Dark Jamaican Rum
2 tblsp. cocoa
2 tblsp. confectioner's sugar
1/2 oz. finely chopped semi-sweet chocolate (optional)

Use a 9-inch spring-form pan sprayed with nonstick spray and dusted with flour. With cake mixer or hand whisk, whip egg whites with a pinch of salt and 1/2 of the sugar. Set aside. Whip the egg yolks with the remaining sugar, rum extract, espresso coffee and beer. Fold in with rubber spatula alternately into egg yolk mixture — 1/3 egg whites, 1/3 flour, cocoa, baking powder, pinch of salt, 1/3 egg whites, etc. (Sift dry ingredients together before adding to yolk mixture.) Pour into spring-form pan and bake in a preheated 315 degree oven for 25 to 35 minutes. Cake is done when it springs back to the touch. Cool on rack.

For filling: In the mixer, add the marscapone cheese, confectioner's sugar and rum extract. Mix for 5 minutes and slowly add heavy cream. Mix 5 minutes more then change to the whisk on the machine. Mix at high until stiff peaks form.

When the sponge cake has cooled, half cake horizontally to form 2 layers. Place the bottom layer back in the pan; top with half of the cream filling. Place other layer, cut side up, on top of bottom layer. Brush with rum, then top with the rest of the filling. Mix cocoa and sugar and sift evenly over top. Add chopped chocolate if desired.

INDEX

A

Almond Cookies 122
Antipasto 25

B

Baked Clams Areginata 29
Baked Stuffed Eggplant 101
Baked Ziti 54
Beef Barley Soup 113
Beef Braciole 89
Beef Stock 12
Beer Batter Fried Fish 67
Boneless Pork Cacciatore 88
Bread 15

C

Caesar Salad 107
Calamari Parmigiano 68
Calamari Scampi 66
Calzone 34
Cannoli 120
Carpaccio 23
Castagnaccio 124
Chicken Areginata 62
Chicken Arricciata 58
Chicken Cacciatore 59
Chicken Paprika 60
Chicken Portuguese 61
Chicken Siciliano 57
Chicken Stock 12
Cold Calamari Salad 106
Cold Eggplant 30
Cold Pasta Salad 105
Cream of Mushroom 114
Cream of Watercress 115

E

Eggplant Milanese 100
Escarole Saute 102

F

Fettucine Carbonara 53
Fettucine Castagnola 52
Fettucine Mia Figlia 53
Flavored Bread Crumbs 14
Flavored Croutons 14
Flavored Flour 14
Flavored Olive Oil 16
Fresh Fruit
   with Rum Sauce 121
Fresh Mozzarella
   and Tomato Salad 27

G

Garlic Bread 24

L

Linguine Aglia Olio 48
Linguine Marinara 45
Linguine Pesto 44
Linguine Primavera 47
Linguine Tutto Giardino 46
Linguine with Chicken 43
Linguine with Clam Sauce . 49

M

Marinara Sauce 13
Meatballs 91
Mushroom Cheese Melt 36

O

Osso Bucco Milanese 86
Oxtails Cacciatore 87

P

Pasta Fagiole 111
Pepper Pot Soup 116
Pesto Sauce 13
Pizza 33
Pizza Bread 24
Pocket Pizza 35
Pork Braciole 89
Port, Wine, Fruit, Cheese
  and Nuts 119
Potatoes Castagnola 99

R

Ricotta Cheesecake 123
Rigatoni Arrabiata 51
Rigatoni Ricotta 50

S

Sausage with Peppers 92
Sauteed Mushrooms 26
Sauteed Zucchini 100
Seafood Baccala 69
Seafood Jambalaya 65
Shrimp in Butter Sauce 28
Shrimp San Marzano 71
Shrimp Scampi 72

T

Tiramisu 125
Tossed Salad 108
Tripe Napolentano 90

V

Veal and Peppers 84
Veal Anna O'Neal 83
Veal Chops with Peppers 85
Veal Francese 82
Veal Marsala 81
Veal Parmigiano 80
Veal Piccata 84
Veal Sorrentino 79
Vegetable Marinade 101
Vichysoisse 112
Vinaigrette Dressing 108

Z

Zabaglione 121
Zapoli 119
Zuppa di Clams
  (or Mussels) 70